MW00979962

Engaging Grace

Engaging Grace

✦

How To Use The Power Of Co-Creation In Daily Life

Rev. Mary E. Schroeder

Writers Club Press
New York Lincoln Shanghai

Engaging Grace
How To Use The Power Of Co-Creation In Daily Life

All Rights Reserved © 2002 by Rev. Mary E. Schroeder

No part of this book may be reproduced or transmitted in any form or by any means, graphic, electronic, or mechanical, including photocopying, recording, taping, or by any information storage retrieval system, without the written permission of the publisher.

Writers Club Press
an imprint of iUniverse, Inc.

For information address:
iUniverse, Inc.
2021 Pine Lake Road, Suite 100
Lincoln, NE 68512
www.iuniverse.com

ISBN: 0-595-25415-2

Printed in the United States of America

Contents

Lesson One: The Basics of Co-Creation

Since the beginning of time, human beings have assumed there was an invisible power greater than they. From cave drawings, to pyramids, to the great cathedrals, people intuitively knew there was some greater power affecting their lives. They gave it names like Ra, the sun god, and created rituals and rites of passage to satisfy the gods in the hope of making life easier. Many of these practices seem kind of bizarre today, but at the time were very logical for their level of understanding and whatever goal they were trying to attain. Today we still feel an inherent desire for freedom from pain or fear, just like those souls eons ago. We intuitively yearn for something that seems intangible. God created us with volition, the ability to make choices. We have volition at every moment. We can choose what we will do, how we will act, what path we will take. It is an awesome gift and, when we really understand it, an awesome responsibility. In my experience, God stands with open arms and says, "Here is your real self and it is wonderful!"

Many people investigate spiritual teachings hoping to find an easy way to avoid life's problems, and think if they could only add a few spiritual practices to their life they would surely find bliss. What does it mean to become more spiritual? Digging around in Webster's I found the definition of *spirituality* as "the quality or state of being spiritual." Looking up *spiritual* it said, "relating to, consisting of, or affecting the spirit." I finally got to the core of this by looking up *spirit*, which in my dictionary has 14 definitions, but the one most appropriate for our topic was "an animating or vital principle held to give life to physical organisms." Now we're getting somewhere.

In the multiple definitions of spirit, it was refreshing not to find it described as supernatural, but instead as "departing from what is usual or normal so as to appear to transcend the laws of nature." Great, because I believe that spirituality does not transcend the law, it is the law of nature. It is the vital principle which gives us life. It is natural—there is nothing supernatural about it. The great spiritual teachers and philosophers of all time discovered that this life is as spiritual as it is going to get. We are already spiritual beings and everything in our life is spiritual. It doesn't take years of study to "get it." Our task as co-creators with God, which is also called the spiritual journey, is to consciously recognize the power of this gift, or as my favorite teacher, Ernest Holmes, called it, The Thing Itself.

In studying spirituality, do you think it is more like an activity you could do after work or on Sundays? The spiritual path is the consciousness we hold every moment during every activity. Living a spiritual life is not something to be done whenever we have time. It is a moment-by-moment practice, a journey where we have the choice of experiencing peace, security, and happiness. At a recent seminar we were asked to repeat something while first moving the right hand in a circle, and then the left hand in a circle. The words were, "I am the creator," then "I am the destroyer." After saying it a few times with the movement, the meaning begins to sink in and I understood how true it is. At any moment I can create a more loving atmosphere or, in the blink of an eye, I can destroy it. The challenge is that no one can make the choice for us; we must make the great discovery for ourselves.

Engaging Grace is a process of opening the heart and mind to your true nature, your real potential. The lessons are tools for your personal journey. Along the way you will more fully understand how to apply the knowledge of the Laws of the Universe for greater good. Over time, using the principles will become a natural part of how you live. This will give you greater confidence and serenity in even the most difficult situations.

The journey called the spiritual path is a process of learning how to use our freedom of choice for our greater good by understanding and aligning with the Laws of the Universe. When we recognize the fact that **God is all that is**, the beauty in every aspect of our life will blossom as we see the divinity in everyone and every place. Opportunities exist in every aspect of our life to enhance our good, whether we are in the grocery store, in line at the bank, walking in the woods, or at a concert. There is no place we can go to get away from the fact that we are spiritual beings in a life experience. This knowledge isn't something that works for us if we just pick it up and hold it. It is through embodiment of principles that you prove to yourself, time and time again, principle works. A spiritual teacher, Ram Dass, says "It is a peculiar predicament that the knowledge can only be known by transforming ourselves into the knowledge itself." The essence of living with a positive mental attitude based on spiritual principles, allows us to live every moment as a life transforming activity.

At the base of every metaphysical class, book, lesson, and principle is one fact: God is all there is. We live in a spiritual Universe with "God" the animating or vital principle, which has given life to all. This creative power is God and this creative essence exists in everything, and therefore, is in, through, and around us. It is in the person sitting next to us, the table, the flower, the bird, the tree.

> *Knowledge of the Truth makes us free by aligning us with that which was never bound.*
>
> —Ernest Holmes
> Living the Science of Mind

The essence of God is expressing Itself throughout all creation. God is for us—It could never be against us or it would self-destruct. Creation operates by law, a changeless principle based on love and God's desire for self-expression through It's creation.

To live with this knowledge is to recognize that behind all events, death and destruction, is harmony, the perfection of the Universe unfolding around us. We will delve deeper into this as we progress, but at the moment, just consider that all people are on their own path consciously or unconsciously. Some travel in pain and anguish, while others live in varying degrees of happiness and contentment. Try experimenting with the idea that each person is in their unique place for this play of life, where whatever their recognition of truth, it is right for them at the moment. Each individual life experience reflects their play of divine consciousness. This brings out a sense of compassion in us, especially when it comes to recognizing the spiritual path in family members. It is one thing to recognize the truth in those we don't know well, but so often we think we can fix family members so they can avoid pain and see life more positively. But there is no difference—their life experience is their play of consciousness. Yet inner change often comes from having a direct experience with others. Each of us is a light and the clearer and brighter our light shines, as we live in the awareness of truth, we become a catalyst for change in others just by being who we are.

Family, job, children, gardening, exercising, playing are all part of this path to greater self-awareness. By embodying more of our co-creative power and living from a basis of spiritual truth, we will naturally be able to hold a stronger consciousness of love and truth in negative circumstances, to be a light in the darkness. We cannot predict what impact this will have on others, but we know the good it does for us.

In walking this path to freedom of fear, be aware of the laws that operate in the Universe. The planet earth, the stars, the sun, the moon, the seasons, the tides, the cycle of birth and death flow in perfect harmony. By studying life and the laws of nature we get a better grasp of what a law is. We see gravity, for instance, works equally on all objects. It doesn't work more powerfully one moment and less the next; the laws of the Universe do not play favorites. Cause and Effect is another principle that impacts every aspect of our life, working perfectly every time. These laws are not supernatural; they don't change over time, they just are. Why a principle exists we will never know. What we can know is how it works and live in alignment with these principles to find freedom, peace, and happiness.

> *The best we can do is become an environment for every person we meet that allows them to open in the optimum way they can.*
>
> —Ram Dass
> Grist For The Mill

Listening is one of the greatest gifts we can give ourselves. Not just listening to others, but listening to our inner voice in total honesty. In reading this chapter, the process has already begun. Actions that come forth from deep listening should be based on: Does the thing I wish to do express more life, more happiness, more peace to myself, and at the same time harm no one? If it fits this description, it is right. If not, it is selfish, and whether it helps or hurts anyone, we will reap the consequences.

As we learn how to live life from a spiritual base, we see that life as a series of falling down and getting up as we learn to make better choices. Each step teaches us more about how this Thing works and how to use it. This is the essence of metaphysics, the study of co-creation. Ernest Holmes explains it as, "the study of First Cause, Spirit, Mind, or that invisible Essence, that ultimate Stuff and Intelligence from which everything comes, the Power back of creation—the Thing Itself." Our efforts to understand the natural laws of Life will result in positive change as we explore and begin to relate to life in alignment with the laws of its own nature. As Holmes described it, nothing moves but mind and by living from that center of knowledge, we taste the nectar of life. We dig deeper and open our mind and heart to reveal our true self, and it is sweet.

In discovering the power of co-creation for ourselves, it helps to understand the principles of how it works so we may be more conscious and aware in daily activities.

This is the simple meaning of true metaphysical teaching, the study of Life and the nature of the Law, governed and directed by thought; always conscious that we live in a spiritual Universe; that God is in, through, around and for us.

—Ernest Holmes
The Science of Mind

PRINCIPLES OF CO-CREATION

(Principle: a fundamental law)

There is One infinite, all-inclusive, creative, living Intelligence beyond and within the Universe. It is God, the Living Spirit Almighty, One indestructible, absolute and self-existent Cause which manifests Itself in and through all creation.

Our essential nature is spiritual; the eternality, the immortality and the continuity of the individual soul, forever expanding.

We have a creative relationship with our experience of life. We are surrounded by Creative Mind, which receives the direct impress of our thought and acts upon it.

Life is a spiritual journey toward an awareness of the true source of our being. The ultimate destiny of every individual soul is to awaken to the true source—God Itself.

BELIEFS ABOUT THE NATURE OF CO-CREATION

(Belief: a state of mind in which trust or confidence is placed)

We are all united in Oneness with God.

The basis of God's creation is Love.

We are free to choose our experience in life every minute.

We find peace when we connect with the Source.

We experience wholeness when we are centered in the knowledge of Oneness with all.

Spiritual growth is the purpose of life on this plane.

Life is best expressed not in the belief in God, but in expressing the love of God.

We find spiritual growth and understanding by taking personal responsibility for understanding everything that happens in our lives.

We recognize universally, all that moves is mind, so we can relate this to the power of prayer. The word "prayer" comes from the Latin word "precarious," meaning obtained by begging, to implore. At some point in life when we were in a tough spot, maybe a prayer came to mind requesting the intercession of God, an angel or saint. If every prayer was answered, this world would be in total chaos since no one would ever get sick or die and God would get tired making someone love one person, then another and then another. Yet we have all had some prayers answered.

If the Universe operates on principle or law, there must be a natural law behind the power of prayer that, when understood, enables us to have a higher percentage of success. In studying the principles of co-creation it has also been found that the process of affirmative prayer follows closely with the processes of creation. The form of affirmative prayer is scientifically based and has proven to be highly successful thousands and thousands and thousands of times. It is presented here and at the end of each chapter for your consideration.

FIVE STEPS IN AFFIRMATIVE PRAYER

1) **RECOGNIZE GOD AS THE ONLY POWER**

- GOD IS…
- God is the source of all, the unlimited power.
- i.e. Declare our definition of God.

2) **UNIFY WITH THAT POWER**

- I AM…
- I am a divine expression of God's desire to express Itself.
- i.e. Declare our spiritual nature, the reality of all people.

3) **DECLARE THE TRUTH IS**

- I KNOW for myself…

4) **THANKSGIVING**

- I GIVE THANKS that I now know…

5) **RELEASE**

Release any doubts and let go of any concerns. Let go and let God, "the Father within," do the work. Now feel and act as if it were so. Declare a strong statement of love and truth, releasing it to the Law to do it's work.

AND SO IT IS! AMEN.

AFFIRMATIVE PRAYER

I AM TOTALLY SUPPORTED

God is the fountain of all thought, the source of the Universe, constantly filling me with its magnificence, creating in me a well of inspiration from which I can drink at any time. I now choose to immerse myself in this fountain, letting its power fill me. I welcome it, I know that it is God.

My life is all about the discovery of my true relationship to God and deepening my inner realization that God's presence and power is always with me. It is about dedicating myself with single-minded purpose to whatever supports me in experiencing more of God in my everyday life. My life is about appreciating who I am and what I do. It is about feeling my own integrity of being, seeing the result of being honest with everyone around me in the most loving way at all times. The Universe responds to me with people who are supportive and honest. With God as my partner, I direct the activities of my life.

Accepting this support as eternally available, I stay clear about what I want in my life. This allows me to make decisions that are good for me. I accept this as part of my personal divine plan in which my intuition, my direct connection with God insures I receive clear answers to my questions. I am in this life experience to grow, expand, absorb, assimilate, and put to use God's knowledge.

In great thanksgiving I recognize that God's good and orderly direction flows through me consciously forevermore. This expresses today as appreciation and self-acceptance. It expands my world and fills it with loving friends and companions. I give thanks and let this new experience unfold with ease and grace. And so it is. Amen.

Lesson Two: The Seed of Perfection

Isn't it just incredible that you are an individual expression of Spirit in action? There has never been anyone like you. You are a divine inspiration of God. God reveals Itself to us through us. It seems extraordinary, doesn't it, that our life comes from a greater power and our daily experience comes from within. One of the primary functions of this book is to consciously connect each one of us with that Universal power.

You've heard, "There is a power for good in the Universe and you can use it." It's true. This Universal Mind, Intelligence, is limitless spiritual substance, not limited to any place in space. The unity of one power without limitation is where metaphysics, whether it is taught in Religious Science, Divine Science, Unity, or other positive living teachings, differs from so many traditional religions. Good is Universal and as much of it as we are able to incorporate into our life is ours to use. Most religions teach God is everywhere present, but often their core belief is that God won't be found just anywhere, but usually in a church or holy place. Could there really be a place where God/Spirit is not? If so, what would be there instead? Although there is much energy focused on the unhappiness and chaos in the world, without unity at the core of it all, our world could not exist for one moment. Attributing unity to good, if we look hard enough, we can see some core level of good in everything, so in times of doubt we must look behind the appearance to find the answer.

We do not have the power of God to move the stars or create a planet, but we do have the ability to align ourselves with this power.

Therefore, some things may seem like they have their own power, such as evil acts, but a belief in good and evil is a belief in duality. Evolving spiritually requires a conscious awareness of the truth—the only law is God's law and nothing opposes it. In *The Anatomy of Healing Prayer*, Holmes says, "Our whole work is based on the concept Perfect God, Perfect Man, and Perfect Being. Our whole practice is based on the concept that God is where we are and what we are, and that there isn't anything else. Our whole concept is partially based on the theory that whatever appears to be wrong is not wrong in itself, but is the wrong arrangement of what is right. There is no dualism in the Universe."

> *The two functions of our spiritual nature are the power to create and the power to experience meaning and purpose.*
>
> —Jacquelyn Small
> Transformers

Since Spirit is limitless, we are not limited. We have an unlimited ability to expand our consciousness. This is the reciprocal relationship between Spirit and each individual. As we open up to universal truths, we find our consciousness expanding. Our desire to fully express life, knowing that we can express in greater ways than ever before, pulls us into a new dimension of understanding. As we open to a greater use of this natural power, the Universe pours into us a greater level of acceptance. Holmes explains in *Observations*, "There is an irresistible push and pull in the Universe which combines to maintain a perfect equilibrium." When we perform our daily tasks in this consciousness, we perform to the best of our ability, and principle sees to its accomplishment. "The Truth known demonstrates Itself."

In us lies the potentiality of everything we shall ever evolve into. Like the laws of our country, ignorance of spiritual laws is no excuse. We evolve at all times whether we consciously make use of the law or not. Ignorance of the law is the cause of all of our troubles. Can you look back at the last problem you had and see a connection between it and a lack of understanding of law, or how a negative belief unfolded through law? A friend of mine could play tennis really well with his right hand and mentioned several times he wanted to learn to play left handed. It wasn't long before he fell and broke his right wrist and was forced to use his left hand. The point is not to think less of ourselves when things happen that appear negative; this is how we learn. Then we move forward and improve our thought patterns so we don't re-create or repeat problems.

When I feel overwhelmed by all of the bad news in the world, I take my mind to the top of Mt. Shasta, a 14,000 foot snow-capped mountain surrounded by forests, lakes and rivers. I feel myself sitting there, looking out over the valley and the cities. I feel a sense of rhythm, a flow of divine harmony as I imagine people coming here from other planes of experience by being born, having a human experience with all of its intricacies, and then going onto another realm by leaving their bodies. It is a divine flow of coming and going, so how could any single experience in this process be less than perfect? In our innermost being lies this seed of perfection.

> *At the center of everything nestles the seed of perfection.*
>
> —Walt Whitman

Often the association we have with our body, our work, or our relationships strongly becomes the essence of who we think we are, our identity. But from the top of Mt. Shasta I see it is our consciousness that has chosen this form on purpose. The inner reality is Spirit in expression, and the outer reality is our individual way of expressing life in this form. The infinite possibilities of how we live in this Universe show up as people involved in war, starvation, famine, parenthood, sickness, disease, teachers, social workers, doctors, waiters, etc. The perfection behind this multitude of appearances is tough for ego mind to grasp, because something that is infinite is beyond our limited mind. Our center of expression comes from our connection with Universal Mind and functions at our level of understanding.

Unity is the one energy behind all things and cannot be multiplied or divided. We live in one infinite whole, omnipresent in its entirety. Judge Thomas Troward said it is logically correct that at every moment all of Spirit is concentrated at any point in space and we may choose to fix our thought upon it and individualize it. Judge Troward (1847–1916) was Her Majesty's Assistant Commissioner and later Divisional Judge of the North Indian Punjab from 1969 until his retirement in 1896. It is at that time he is best remembered and most celebrated for his works on metaphysical studies. He saw the relationship between Spirit and matter as that between idea and form. Spirit is conscious and therefore must be conscious of something. Through contemplation it is creative. As individuals, we all share the reality of unity at a core level, yet are free to express diversity at our conscious level. When we were in the first grade of school, our ability to see all that we would learn by the time we graduated was very limited. Our acceptance of the nature of diversity is clearer when we are in an airport or shopping mall observing the variety of shapes, sizes, and personalities, yet recognizing each one is perfect, since each person is expressing life as only they know how.

Recognizing our ability to grasp our unity with God, with Spirit, is limited by what we have learned and embodied so far. As you progress through this book, you will know and understand more, but most importantly you will have a greater ability to use this knowledge daily in practical ways. The valleys we experience as we grow won't be so dark as we live with a deeper understanding and love for all aspects of life. By loving the highs and lows, the result will be greater harmony and inner peace as we flow with the divine energy in life. As Holmes says, "We shall find a better God when we shall have arrived at a higher standard for man."

Contemplation: What is Spirit's agenda in my life?

The philosophy of co-creation offers a clear path of empowerment that gives us the knowledge of how to deal with any question or situation in life. All we deal with is mind. Implicit confidence and faith in the Law are the chief requirements for effectively using it. We experience this truth not just by reading about it, but by proving it to ourselves. Deeper understanding comes from being around people who are also in contact with their spiritual energy. Associating with others on this path helps to reinforce the importance of contemplation, affirmative prayer, meditation, and watching our thoughts and actions. As we get stronger in our understanding and use of principles, we will have more conscious experiences of grace. Simply making the effort to participate through study increases our awareness level. In recognizing this natural flow of life and feeling at ease with it, our presence becomes a light for others.

Since the nature of the Universe is to always say "yes" and give us what we believe, if we think we are not worthy of a high-paying job, one won't be offered to us. If we believe we are not attractive, we find ourselves with people who verify this. When we say something negative about someone else, the Universe hears "yes" and brings it back to us for our experience. Just as negative beliefs come back to us in negative ways, so do positive beliefs. By frequently checking our mind, we can determine whether our dominant thoughts, feelings, beliefs, are helping or hurting us. Look at your thoughts today. If you were to place a black dot on paper for every negative thought you have had so far, how many dots would there be? Ironically "the power which appears to bind us is the only power in the Universe which can free us." Our thoughts of unworthiness bind us, yet when these thoughts are changed to worthiness, the Universe again responds "YES!" How perfect!

One area that shows us our conscious or unconscious use of this power is relationships. Most of us desire a loving, supportive relationship. By law our natural power of attraction draws to us the perfect person who mirrors our deepest beliefs about ourselves. Relationships mirror our most intense feelings, which is why it is so easy to see what we believe. This can be wonderful or very disturbing. Relationships show us parts of ourselves we don't like and parts we are proud of. Often, instead of recognizing the reflection as something we need to change inside ourselves, we blame the other person for not bringing to the relationship the qualities we feel we deserve. When we feel a person is unloving, it is because there is a place in us that is unloving. If we look at what we want to change in our relationships, knowing it is done unto us as we believe, it really isn't too tough to identify what needs to change in us. Admitting it is the first step. In order to make a friend, we must be a friend. To have a warm and loving relationship, we must be a warm and loving person. Our belief sets our limitation in relationships and everything else. The apparent blocks on our path to happiness are thereby our sense of limitation or lack.

You don't see the center of the Universe because it's all center.

—C. S. Lewis

Reflecting on your life today, can you identify your most deeply held beliefs? What do you think they are? Look closely and examine each thoroughly. Do you deserve more good than this? "As much as we can believe will be done unto us." If you see several areas for improvement, choose one to focus on this month. As you work positively on this area, other aspects of life will automatically shift. In all activities of life we find this Law of Perfection. If we plant tomato seeds and add water, the reaction of the seed with the water in the soil will soon result in tomato plants. If duality existed, we could not expect a particular outcome; tomato seeds might result in carrots or weeds. Since Law is mechanical, if we're too busy to water the tomato plants, they will naturally shrivel up. The Universe won't step in to save them just because we are doing something else. We are dealing with an impersonal law which says: no water, no tomato plants. Plants do not have volition, the ability to choose, like we do. Plants cannot decide they need water and crawl over to the hose and turn it on. Its life is a mechanical, natural event, which is impacted by many things in its growth cycle.

Personal empowerment is a major result of understanding the Laws of the Universe. If we want to change our life for the better starting right now, we can. "Change your thinking, change your life!" By changing Cause, our thoughts and beliefs, we can change the Effect we experience. In *The Science of Mind*, Holmes writes, "We are thinking, willing, knowing, conscious centers of Life. We are surrounded by, immersed in, and there is flowing through us, a creative Something...call It what you will. The sum total of all our thought, will, purpose, and belief, creates a tendency in this Law that causes It to react to us according to the sum total of that belief." The power which appears to bind us is the only power that can free us, so when we look closely we see that suffering is created by ignorance of the Law.

If the reason we are here is the self-expression of God, than each person, place, and thing is important to the unity of the Whole. The greater harmony in the Whole, surely the greater expression of life in each of its parts. At the molecular level, each part is made up of particles with atoms, which, when combined with other atoms, takes on a multitude of forms. The smallest particle has an inherent perfection and is in pure harmony in its own way. As particles combine and build into the multitude of expressions we see in the Universe, we could not remove part of these building blocks and expect a form to stay the same. Each individual expression of life, including our life, is significant to the whole. The world would be diminished if we weren't here. As we expand and grow in knowledge and our ability to use the Laws of the Universe for a greater good, it contributes to the further progression and expression of the Whole.

> *Until we are enlightened, all action must be an exercise in working on our own consciousness.*
>
> —Ram Dass

Troward encourages us to go for greater expression in *The Law and the Word*, "Once we grasp this idea of the unity and progressiveness of Life going on *ad infinitum*, what boundless vistas of possibility open before us. It would be enough to stagger the imagination were it not for our old friends, the Law and the Word. But these will always accompany us, and we may rely upon them in all worlds and under all conditions."

It is comforting to know that our spiritual growth depends on taking a step in consciousness from a tangible and limited God to an intangible, unlimited Mind. With personal strength and persistence, we can consciously work to embody the attributes of Spirit which allows us to express life more fully. When we take a step in this direction, shift happens. As we get positive results, it means we are digging deeper inside to root out beliefs that create negative experiences. Spiritual practices that help us overcome those beliefs include daily affirmative prayer, spiritual readings, contemplation, and meditation. Daily spiritual practice is the reinforcement for positive change as new cause is set into motion. By recognizing a belief in conscious mind, we take the power of negative thinking away and erase its destructive possibilities. Consistent spiritual practices accumulate positive images and impressions, which, over time, outweigh any leftover residuals of negative thought.

We develop the realization of the truth found in metaphysics as, time after time, we prove to ourselves affirmative prayer and living in principle works. "I think I can, I think I can," said the little engine to itself as it climbed the steep hill and made it to the top. "Whatever the mind can conceive, we can achieve," whether it be to do good or harm, to help or hurt, to give or take. At both ends of the scale the Law works consistently. This is the seed of perfection. Holmes explained, "We experience good and evil because we perceive a presence of duality rather than unity." Our thoughts create the appearance of two sides battling for success, but spiritual practices work to bring our thoughts to peace and harmony. Reaching for a higher good is worthwhile. Take time today to reveal the inner goodness that is yours.

If you meditate on your ideal, you will acquire its nature. If you think of God day and night, you will acquire the nature of God.

—Sri Ramakrishna

DIALOGUE

Freedom to me means I can do what I want, when I want, which sounds good. So I'm confused when you say metaphysics believes we are free, yet these lessons and lectures sound like rules on how to live "in principle."

As unique creations of God, we are free to choose what we want to do, when, and how. We can choose to bring ourselves pain or pleasure in the moment or in the future. It is a big responsibility to decide between immediate gratification vs. our long term good. And it is also our nature to want to be loved. Therefore, living in a way to bring more love and pleasure into our life, means we live in a way that expresses <u>more</u> life, <u>more</u> happiness, <u>more</u> peace, **and harms no one**, and that includes us. Using this criteria as a litmus test for living in principle, love becomes the basis for our full expression of freedom.

I've been doing spiritual practices every day, but still I get impatient or upset over things. When will this end so I can just be peaceful and happy?

When we have worked free of a negative habit or behavior, it is easy to have expectations of never being tempted by it again. Wouldn't that be great! I love the way Ram Dass talks about this. He says we never fully lose our neurosis—instead they become like little schmoozes that sneak up when we feel free, tickle us and say, "Are you really done with this one?" And we find out if we really have the confidence and spiritual maturity to just shoo it away. Life is a creative process in which we are constantly evolving. This is the stuff of the Universe, so maintaining peace and love in our life is a continual process. Troward believed this is evolution, an upward spiral motion where our best experiences will come by being consciously involved in creating and expanding a meaningful and fulfilled life.

The more I learn about metaphysics, I find it hard to believe I am totally responsible for my life. Abusive spouse, intimidating boss...if I am free, why would I choose this?

First we must go back to Unity and understand that without Unity throughout the Universe, we would not exist. The basis of all things manifested is God in expression. In our life, there are two agendas going on at all times: the Big Agenda and the Little Agenda. The Big Agenda is spirit's agenda regarding what we learn and how we grow in this lifetime. Can you see the Big Agenda in the life of Jesus, Mother Teresa, Helen Keller, Pope John Paul? The Little Agenda is our conscious agenda, our responsibility for how we want to do life. Know that as we grow spiritually, we will recognize our life circumstances can be changed internally and externally. We will find the conscious strength to move ourselves out of situations that do not support us in a positive and life-affirming way. If we just take whatever comes, life shouts at us many times in negative ways to grow, learn, and make better choices.

AFFIRMATIVE PRAYER

GRACE UNFOLDS IN MY LIFE NOW

The Infinite Mind of God permeates and moves through all things. The energy of God is a constant state of love, which is always finding new ways to express. This love is the natural essence of every being and every thing. It is the center of what I call my life.

As a unique expression of God's infinite love, I recognize how my life experiences are guided by Law. As I give, I receive. The love and tenderness I give to others returns to me in ways much greater than I could have anticipated. It is how all things work. Therefore, I focus my life on being honest with myself and others and living at the highest level of integrity. This allows the abundant grace of God to flow in all areas of my life. I accept now that all of my wants and needs are fulfilled. My heart center now resides in a great state of inner peace. No matter what face I see or emotion I feel, I know at the center of every being there is perfect Spirit, perfect love, perfect God. This is the key that unlocks the door to happiness. My heart opens wide at this recognition and grace pours forth as I see beyond any condition.

I give great thanks for this recognition of the power of living life with integrity and love. It is an aspect of me that I give unconditionally, knowing it returns to me in greater measure. As a result, there is now more honesty, integrity, and love in my life. It is the Law of the Universe and it is working in very powerful ways.

I release and let go of any concern or doubt about how the Law works as I embrace the creative, perfect nature of God. Grace unfolds forever more in my life in positive and supportive ways. And so it is. Amen.

Lesson Three: The Power of Love Through Law Has No Limits

Have you felt the creative power of the Universe today? This is the power behind all things, all movement and motion. Every individual form of expression is a manifestation of God's divine love. Just our recognition of this vast source of love can awaken an energy within that goes beyond our normal comprehension.

Feelings of love require expression, which can show up in many creative ways. Trust your own intuition when you feel this urge. It is directing you to an experience of bliss. It may say take the right turn instead of the left at the next corner, where you then may catch sight of a hawk in flight, a baby lamb scampering across a field, children playing, geese flying overhead, an array of wildflowers along the side of the road. Little blessings like these warm our hearts and let the soul's energy release with love. If intuition encourages us to do something, whether it is planting flower bulbs, riding a bike, writing a letter to an old friend, or using a new recipe for dinner, these creative acts are gifts of love. By giving ourselves the experience of love, a genuine inner transformation takes place. Allow this surge of energy to come into our consciousness and permeate our experience. When we connect with the power of love in the soul, it is a time for joy.

> *In order to love, one must think about love, one must deeply contemplate love, one must create a bond of friendship with love.*
>
> —Swami Muktananda
> From the Finite to the Infinite

The Bible says, "Who knows not love knows not God; for God is love." As metaphysicians, we believe that love is the greatest energy in the Universe. Without the energy of love, what would we feel when we observe something beautiful? At birth our first need is for love, and it is the last need when we die. In and of itself love is a tremendous healing power. Feeling wanted, needed, and loved mends any hurt and dries any tear. Have you observed a child who falls and is instantly healed with a hug and a kiss? Why would we ever intentionally hold back such a power? When we hold back our love, it is pure selfishness.

Selfishness is based in a deep belief in lack, a belief there is not enough of what we want, whether it is love, food, friendship, money, recognition or something as basic as confidence. When we hang this padlock around our heart, there is little energy left to focus on others and no room left for grace to flow in, which in turn blocks our ability to receive love. One of the things I suggest to people who feel they don't have enough love in their life or their life has no value, is to do selfless service by volunteering to help others or organizations in a consciousness of love, expecting nothing in return. The act of giving to those in need opens the heart, guaranteed. Selfishness cannot exist when love and compassion rule our heart.

There is a method for discovering inner love, which begins with doing acts of loving kindness for the self. Start by remembering a time in your life when you did receive love. Perhaps it was from a parent, a grandparent, friend or neighbor. Visualize that special moment when you felt so loved and appreciated. Let the warmth of their energy rise in your heart as you reflect on the words or actions that bring that sense of bliss. Now let the loving kindness you feel go out to the person who gave you love. It is clear, you are worthy of love and they are worthy of love. This is how the power of love works, through giving and receiving. Now in your mind, give love to other people close to you, using the power of thought, know love is abundant for friends and neighbors, strangers, and those that may hurt you. In this exercise you give love to your soul and to God by giving love to all of those people who are individual ways God expresses.

Another step in opening your heart to love is by recognizing other people are just the same as you. As the Dalai Lama said, "After all, all human beings are the same—made of human flesh, bones, and blood. We all want happiness and want to avoid suffering. Further, we have an equal right to be happy. It is important to realize our sameness as human beings." We are all spiritual beings going through a human experience.

All is love and yet all is Law. Love rules through Law.
Love is the Divine Givingness; Love is the Way.
Love is spontaneous; Law is impersonal.

—Ernest Holmes
The Science of Mind

True love begins with the self. Do you love yourself? Think about the last time you stood in front of a mirror and said, "I love you!" If it has been awhile, make sure you do it today. Stare straight into your eyes until you can smile. Experience the cosmic giggle of Spirit who brought the cells of your body together in this form. See the beauty, the unique beauty God has given you. Your life is a divine expression of the One.

We all need to love ourselves, for how can we honestly love others if we lack the belief that we are worthy of our own love? If self-love is a challenge for you, consider the Law of Cause and Effect: Our beliefs cause our experience. If I have love in my heart for myself, you can feel it just by being around me. Often we are happy to meet someone who is at ease, who appears very relaxed and smiles easily. It feels good to be around people like this because their atmosphere has no anxiety, tension, or worry. It helps to be around positive and loving people and feel our desire to share those characteristics. But we fool ourselves if we hope that just by being around them something, like magic, will rub off on us. What they have comes from inside, which is exactly where we will find the answer. Their gift is a light of love that shines so bright we find it irresistible. If that is what we want, our job is to do whatever necessary to allow our light to shine as brightly. We begin right where we are, sharing the power of love from our hearts one step at a time.

If there is someone in your life who is difficult to love, try transplanting your love; put yourself in the shoes of that person. It is easy to love those who love us, but we have a greater gift to give. God's love comes through us when we feel compassion for others. Growth comes from loving what the ego perceives as the unlovable. If you were this unlovable person, how would you like to be treated? How would you like to be loved? Transplanting our feet into their shoes helps us let go of ego mind and replace it with compassion. Compassion is the part of us that sees the rocky road someone has created and the pain that comes with it, and yet knows there is an answer, a way to get back to the smooth highway of life. Find a place of understanding in your heart for what that person has experienced in their life. Feel it and let compassion swell in your heart. Understand, accept and let go of negative feelings. We are all the same in the eyes of God, so be open to the grace of compassion by giving love.

Love is our highest word and the synonym of God.

—Ralph Waldo Emerson
Essay on Love

What we long for the most is love from other people, yet there never seems to be enough. We take it so personally when someone doesn't love us THIS MUCH. When our attention centers on us, we want everyone's attention—see me, hear me, love me. One teacher said we all want someone else to give us love, to make our life exciting and blissful every day, but seldom do we want to be the person who must give, give, and give, day in and day out to make that happen. When someone finds it hard to show love, even in a simple form of friendship or respect for a stranger, they are deeply caught in their own feelings, pulled so far inward there is no awareness or capacity to do anything else. They live in an illusion that has nothing to do with us, it is just where they are in their personal growth. If we can be a light of love, we might be the catalyst for them to open and risk changing.

When we are receiving love, we may forget to give love in return. By giving some expression of love, saying a few words or a smile, we can balance the flow and enrich the experience. Look around. Where would a smile or a kind word help someone? One place where it is fun to give love is the grocery store, where many people walk by oblivious of those around them. Be conscious while you shop. Catch someone's eye and smile. To me a smile says, "I recognize you as a worthy person, as God in its many forms of expression. And so it is."

Just like all things, the Law of Cause and Effect rules love. When we give love, we receive a response and we cannot receive love without having a response. It is the nature of love to be irresistible and transform everyone it touches in some way. In *The Science of Mind*, we read, "Love is an essence, an atmosphere, which defies analysis, as does Life Itself. It is that which IS and cannot be explained; it is common to all people, to all animal life, and evident in the response of plants to those who love them. Love reigns supreme over all." Like the lamp that dissipates the darkness, love can overcome hate, fear and sadness.

Whether our life has been fascinating or devastating, the world is as we see it. We create our heaven or hell, yet all of it is the divine expression of Spirit. Our greatest gift in this life is choice; we can choose to do life different from this point forward. What would you like to do different from now on? A powerful way to move forward is by daily spiritual practices. There are many to choose from, but the most important thing is to begin. Set aside time every day, even 5 minutes to start, to connect with Spirit and Universal Mind. Through meditation we get in touch with this space between our thoughts, beyond the ego mind, which starts the day in peace and clarity. At first disturbing thoughts or regrets for past deeds may fill our mind, but it is Spirit's way of showing us areas that need our love. By taking 20–30 minutes each morning to connect with Spirit and feel ourselves resting in the arms of God, the day flows much easier. We project such happiness when we are centered in our love of God. If we don't take time to reach the silence, it is very easy to find drama at every turn and get caught up in the perceived misery of the world. We begin to let go of this trap by daily meditation, spiritual reading, and the contemplation of love, love of self and others.

> *For most of your life you've lived at the effect of your experiences. Now you're invited to be the cause of them. That is what is known as conscious living. That is what is called walking in awareness.*
>
> —Neale Donald Walsch
> Conversations With God

If we describe love as a strong affection, caring, concern, tenderness, and benevolence, to have an abundance of love and freely give it away would be to live in a state of bliss. This is the highest state, to recognize the divinity in every person, place or thing, and to feel love for it all. The central core of the Universe is love. In the Bible Jesus said, "I say to you, love your enemies, bless those who curse you, do good to those who hate you, and pray for those who spitefully use you and persecute you, that you may be sons of your Father in Heaven; for He makes His sun rise on the evil and on the good, and sends rain on the just and on the unjust." Matthew 5:44–45. The Law works the same for everyone.

In his book *Sex, Ecology, Spirituality,* Ken Wilbur discusses a multi-dimensional Universe with an interwoven pattern of Ascending and Descending love, called Eros and Agape. In the time of Plato and Plotinus, this was a doctrine in which love played the central part. Eros is the ascending love, the love of the lower reaching up to the higher. Agape is the love of the higher reaching down to care for the lower. As we express more ascending love, the Universe reaches down to us from a higher level with compassion and grace, helping us to respond with even greater love, which pulls us into an even higher dimension, thus the pattern of expansion. Ascending love results in a vast expansion of love throughout the Universe. Thomas Troward talked about a reciprocal relationship between Spirit and the Individual where, as we open up, the Universe pours itself into us, resulting in expanded individualization of consciousness, somewhat like the sun's light pulling on a plant to grow and show its inner beauty. It all begins on the inside.

> *Love allows a person to see the true angelic nature of another person, the halo, the aura of divinity.*
>
> —Thomas Moore
> Care of the Soul

We can't give what we don't have. If our hearts are closed and love is not forthcoming, we are not open to receive love either. This is a challenge for single people as they meet others in anticipation of finding the perfect loving relationship, commonly referred to as the RPM, our "right and perfect mate." When I was at this stage after a lengthy marriage and divorce, I was confused about how to decide when someone I met was possibly "the one" I had been waiting for. My teacher was very clear with me on this subject. He said my job was to be fully present and in love (obviously not intimate love) with every person I meet, to totally be myself and let God handle the details. He said the men that could not handle this love, honesty, and clarity would leave, and the one who could appreciate and honor that love would stay. It was scary. I have an innate desire to please others, but now it was time to just be me and it worked. Yes, it takes courage to open our heart and allow others to see our weaknesses and our strengths.

What we really want is people in our life who love us for being natural and who support us with their love. By being open and honest we experience the tenderness and the pain in the world. This is living. Our heart is touched and compassion blossoms. Holmes explains, "A life that has not loved has not lived, it is still dead." We cannot experience the gifts of the Universe if we have not developed our ability to love, because the Universe is based on love. Inner love is awakened by grace and its source is our own self. The source of all love is within and can be released through the expansion of grace resulting from doing spiritual practices.

When we maintain an atmosphere of love in any situation, the Law of Mental Equivalents brings us the experience of love as a reaction in our body. If you are a caregiver, nurse, police officer, teacher, or anyone who is in an environment where you are the "helper," watch out for the trap of being too formal and distant with the ones you are helping. The problem of being a helper is not the work, but our identification with it. The ego enjoys being in a helping situation by trying to organize it, saying, "I'm the helper, the one with knowledge and skill, and you are the one I am helping, so be quiet and listen to me." Instead of valuing the present moment and the gift each experience holds for us, we try to control the environment and the ways we might help. Our ego forms a picture of our self-image and the more we hold onto it, the more we alienate and diminish the people we try to help. By being an open vessel of love, the actions of being the helper are flavored with an energy that, as Ram Dass says, allows us to meet each other behind our roles, acknowledging our true identities as individual expressions of God, which adds richness to the experience.

Contemplation: Do I see God and Love in all things?

Is God really just love? God must be love and only love or the duality would destroy us. The opposite of love is fear. Love overcomes all fear and cures all fear. Try it. Prove it to yourself. Love is more powerful than any bad feelings we can have for one another. Love softens our heart and reveals our inner beauty. We may try to attribute love and fear with God, but if both emotions were aspects of God, it would be chaos. God is only love. The Universe emanates love and support for all we do and all we want by saying "YES" to our desires and beliefs, so the more we embody the purity of this love, the more beautiful our life becomes.

We know God as all there is. God knows this also. It knows nothing other than Itself as Truth, Love, Cause and Effect with Love at the core of all creation. Love begets love through Law. In giving love we naturally receive love and the inner peace it brings. Begin today!

DIALOGUE

I understand the concept that we experience what we believe, but I believe I am a worthy and loving person and yet I don't attract the type of friends who love me the way I want to be loved and appreciated. What can I do?

Feeling worthy of love is very important because it opens the heart to accepting love. Yet it seems you have some expectations that are getting in the way of both giving and receiving love. When we expect the love we desire will come from particular people in a particular way, we are being too specific; we are not allowing the Universe to bring us our greater good, a greater expression of love and support.

One of my favorite teachers said we should only draw an outline of our desires and hand the paintbrush to God. Let God color in the picture, because God always colors outside the lines to give us something greater than our limited mind could conceive. When we place expectations on our desire, we limit the flexibility of the Universe to provide a greater demonstration.

Another aspect to this question is having expectations of those who do love us, but have a hard time expressing it. Each person has the ability to give love, but not everyone has the capacity to love us as we want to be loved. Depending on where they are in their personal growth, their ability to fulfill your desire may be very limited. Compassion is calling you to love this person even more, regardless of their ability to return that love. Trust in the Law can help. The Law of Cause and Effect is in operation at every moment. If we give love to someone, it does not mean that specific person will give that amount of love back to us. We will get it back, but if we are open to our greater good, we let God decide where that love will come from. Again, expectations can cut short our natural path to greater love.

AFFIRMATIVE PRAYER

I IDENTIFY WITH GOD

The power in the Universe is the only power and contains all that is required to fulfill its own purpose. This power is always ready to pour into my experience all that I need to succeed and be happy. As I become a channel for God and allow this energy to flow unobstructed through me, good is manifested in my outer experience.

Recognizing the power of identifying with God in my life, I clean out the negative debris I have stored within myself. Every insecure, fearful, self-doubting pattern and belief that separates me from this truth is eliminated from my subconscious right here and now. I do not tread over the past, nor do I use yesterday as an excuse for not living totally today. Being in touch with the divine light in myself, I know it is safe to express all that I think, feel and know, since it comes from my Source and it teaches me about me. I totally accept this process and understand it is part of my experience to love and accept myself just the way I am.

In great thanksgiving I yield my every insecurity to God's sustaining love. I move forward in a positive way knowing this Divine Presence guides me into every experience necessary for my highest good. Sure of who and what I am, I bless myself and all in my world. I let life unfold in perfection, love, and peace. And so it is. Amen.

Lesson Four: Trusting The Invisible

The principles of co-creation may seem very intangible to anyone first studying this philosophy. The theory that we become what we believe according to Law is fascinating, but when we actually see it working in our life, it can be good news or bad news. We might look at our life and think, "Wow, I believe this?!?" Working through our thoughts and beliefs, the Law is always ready and willing to take form as our everyday experience.

The knowledge that life is a mirror of our beliefs has been around for centuries, but there is an undercurrent in society that greatly resists that fact. It is much easier to buy into a philosophy that makes others responsible for our problems. When we aren't happy with life, it may seem too overwhelming, practically impossible for us to change what we've believed for so long. Many authors have presented these ideas in easier-to-swallow concepts. Years ago Napolean Hill wrote a very popular book, *How to Think and Grow Rich.* He believed in the power of autosuggestion, repeating prosperity affirmations to ourselves, which would, through the Law of Prosperity, show up in our experience. He described it like this, "Thoughts that are mixed with any of the feelings of emotions constitute a 'magnetic' force, which attracts other similar or related thoughts." In metaphysics we call this the Law of Attraction, which we know is not some sci-fi sounding invisible force, but an actual law, a principle. In attracting money, Hill described how our mind attracts vibrations, which harmonize with dominant thoughts, so by repeatedly holding thoughts of prosperity, we attract prosperity.

Like metaphysics, he went on to state that when we know prosperity is ours, believe it and trust in it, we attract it by Law.

> *The wisdom of God can do no more for you than it can do through you.*
>
> —Alan Cohen
> I Had It All The Time

Since 1960 Hill and W. Clement Stone sold millions of copies of their book, *Success Through a Positive Mental Attitude.* Their focus on the power of a positive attitude struck a chord throughout society. Their premise was that we are the masters of our fate because we are the masters of our attitude. A positive attitude gets us moving and propels us in the direction we want to go, while a negative attitude sets up inertia, which slows us down and diverts our attention from achieving the goal. Negative thoughts pass through our mind quite frequently, but the trick is not to get caught holding them, but instead let them pass and, more powerfully, consciously replace them with positive thoughts. I suspect that millions of people have used these ideas over the years. Dr. Craig Carter, a metaphysical minister, taught, "When things go wrong, say something right," so when negative thoughts come around, think something right. Our thoughts and words are the creative process, so be aware, and, as Ernest Holmes described, "…feel as though the whole power of the universe were running through the words we speak," because it is. Can you feel it? Do you see how amazing it is that you are powerful enough to actually create your life experiences?

Life in the Universe is expanding, growing, flourishing. All around us we see the Law of Growth in action. Regardless of the exquisite beauty in a rose, as sweetly as it smells, eventually it withers and then another takes its place as the bush expands and flourishes. Nature is always expanding and creating something new with greater complexity and splendor. We also expand and experience a greater life when we grow within ourselves. Inner growth is the way we evolve. It requires letting go of behavior patterns or lifestyles we've been clinging to out of safety and familiarity. Growth cannot occur when we hold on too tightly. By letting go, we release the old ways and create a vacuum into which the Universe brings a new and greater experience.

One area where it is easy to see this law at work is in relationships. If we hold onto a personal relationship that isn't what we want, but feels safe, there is no room for Mister or Misses right to enter our life. By letting go of what does not serve us, a vacuum is created into which we put our thoughts and desires. We make space for a greater relationship to show up in our life. Without focusing our thoughts and desires, without using affirmative prayer and the power of Universal Mind, a vacuum is always filled, filled with whatever happens to come along. Holmes explains it as a fluent force forever taking form and forever deserting the form it has taken. We can mold the direction of growth by using our personal power, so we don't just take whatever comes.

Matter is Spirit at its lowest level.

—Thomas Troward

Living by understanding and applying metaphysical principles on a day-to-day basis gives us direct experiences of our innate power. This growth won't happen if we wait around for friends or neighbors to approve of us or our life. Are there any no-growth areas in your life? Our desires show the way we want to grow and through spiritual practices, Spirit can show us how to make it happen. Working with metaphysical principles we find our power center, knowing the Law is infinite and occupies all space. It fills every form with a differentiation of Itself. It will bring whatever is necessary into our experience so it unfolds perfectly. What has been brought into your life lately that may have been unexpected? Can you see the perfection?

Real power is when we have a consciousness of power to overcome the obstacles we have put on our path. We overcome obstacles by having more courage than fear. Fear develops from negative thoughts, which we can label "False Evidence Appearing Real." Courage is taking positive action in an atmosphere that appears negative, knowing that when we work with the Law, we get results, perfect results. Law works perfectly even when we operate from fear. We can sabotage our good with a belief that our creative power is limited, for instance, by material form. Any belief in limitation discounts the impact of our affirmative prayer, and it works by manifesting as a limited belief. Holmes explained "…if we believe that It will not work, It really works by appearing to 'not work.' When we believe that It cannot and will not, then, according to the principle, It DOES NOT. But when It does not, it still does—only It does according to our belief that It will not." By doubting how the Law works, it works by appearing not to work. Have you had that experience—said a affirmative prayer and in no time a little doubt creeps in and all of a sudden the affirmative prayer appears to not be working? It works by appearing not to work, which is our belief.

One analogy is that by living in fear or any belief of limitation, we are standing on the hose of grace, which waters our life. God is the water tap and the water is always turned on. We engage grace in our life by the use of spiritual practices, positive thoughts and beliefs and affirmative prayer, therefore, the water flows. But if we stand on the hose or kink it through negativity or limited belief, we slow down and can even stop the flow of grace, the flow of water on our garden of life. Spiritual practices give us courage and help us locate and unravel the kinks, so we become more aware of when we are stepping on the hose.

> *Since the world responds by corresponding, all work begins and ends in the self.*
>
> —Dr. Raymond Charles Barker

Sometimes the message that we are stepping on the hose and limiting the flow of grace in our life will come from others when we aren't paying attention or listening close enough to recognize the problem. Work, home, children, bills, all wrapped together can keep us running through life at a fast pace. It is easy to get so caught up in our own stuff we gloss over what is being said. We bounce back and forth between listening and judging others (nothing difficult about that), but if we are willing to examine thoughts of irritation, judgement and joy, we can deepen our understanding of how beliefs shape our experience and begin to listen with new ears. No matter how skilled we become, our thoughts call out to us for a greater experience in life, a continual upward spiral.

Take a personal inventory in the areas of work, health, prosperity, and relationships to see where you might have posted a "No Growth" sign, where you might be stuck in a rut. Are you ready to take the sign down and move on? If you are not sure, you will find out where change is needed by paying attention. Do you ever feel this in meditation? We get our mind quiet and a thought comes floating by trying to distract us. Ram Dass, a wise meditation teacher, says there is a place in our mind where we can watch our thoughts go by. Visualize a pure blue sky. A bird flies by. We can follow the bird, a thought, or stay with the sky. By staying with the sky we allow intuition, our inner voice, to surface and bring solutions to problems into our consciousness without much effort. Experience is the best teacher. Listening to the still, small voice within is surrender based on trust. We trust that in reality all is well and the answer to any of our questions will be given at the right time. In that place of spacious awareness the immensity of any situation will stay in its proper perspective.

Harmony is our basic nature, so when life is not harmonious our goal is to be able to look at a wrong condition knowing we can change it. We can do this through affirmative prayer. Affirmative prayers are things, just like thoughts are things, which through principle, Law, will shift our experience. Again we can prove this by doing affirmative prayer, maintaining the belief, and then by paying attention, watching for a new level of harmony in our life.

Recently a friend of mine was out of a job and lamented how hard it would be to find another good paying job. Of course the Universe said

"YES" to this belief, and the result was my friend put a tremendous amount of effort into finding new employment.

> *Spirit creates by Self-contemplation;*
> *Therefore, what it contemplates itself as being, that it becomes.*
> *You are individualized Spirit;*
> *Therefore, what you contemplate as the Law of your being*
> *becomes the Law of your being.*
>
> —Thomas Troward
> The Creative Process in the Individual

The other day I was driving to a meeting with a friend, and as we approached the location, she commented how impossible it is to find a parking space close to the building. Gently I used a phrase I learned long ago, "That's not my experience," knowing the perfect spot near the building was always easily available, and it was. It takes effort to be aware of all the thoughts zooming through our minds each minute. How many of your thoughts are affirmative and positive? If the pattern is overloaded with negatives, consciously shift the balance to positive and build from there. One way is to catch those negative thoughts and immediately say to yourself, "No, that's not my experience."

Our thoughts create a more forceful result when we have positive thoughts that are powerful, that have a sense of completion in mind. One way to do this is to add words, such as, "This is a beautiful room…that brings joy and happiness to all who enter." Take a positive thought and create a Power Thought. Through this process we develop a picture of the result and tag it onto the initial thought. It can become a natural process in our mind that can be used to turn an average thought into a Power Thought.

I heard someone say "This is terrible!" and then one second later, " Oh, cancel, cancel, cancel that thought!" Obviously there was recognition that the negative statement wasn't what they wanted in their experience, so they tried to cancel it. But was the first thought the real belief? Clear beliefs are the most powerful. A clear belief in positive results can also be achieved by denying any false condition that opposes our desires. "The law of the Lord is perfect." (Psalms 19:7) By being conscious of our belief and outlining our expectations, all we have to do is give it to the Law, which works perfectly every time. Holmes taught, "We do not put the power into this word, but do let the power of the Law flow through it, and the one who most completely believes in this power will produce the best results."

By using Power Thoughts we give more definition to our belief and the Universe responds more directly to us. It is wise to consider how we word our desires. For instance, if a man desires a relationship with a woman and says in mind, "I am in a loving relationship with a 5'7" slim and beautiful redhead," many important things were left out of the desire, such as a woman who is compassionate, truthful, joyful, spiritual, and honest. Many people suggest we make a list about the qualities we desire in a relationship, but always remember the Law will respond perfectly. It is much more satisfying to focus our desire on the 'heart' parts and let God decide the outer form. What has been your experience with this?

> *Behind every condition is a belief, and if you can change the belief, you can change the condition.*
>
> —Dr. Craig Carter

One of the special gifts in the world of metaphysics is Licensed Practitioners, advanced students who offer their service to others in order to help uncover the cause of negative experiences or effects, who work to carve a new path into consciousness in harmony with Law. The process is called Spiritual Mind Healing. Affirmative prayer is the tool used for healing and its level of demonstration is based on each individual's recognition of truth. Three important qualities are necessary for spiritual mind healing: persistence, flexibility, and patience, which releases the Law to work at each individual's own level of acceptance. A guaranteed specific result is not expected with affirmative prayer, because affirmative prayer puts a new cause into motion, and by Law a new effect unfolds. Since cause is the sum total of the person's beliefs and attitudes, the way in which affirmative prayer will demonstrate is not predictable. We know truth is superior to the condition that is to be changed. This belief in ultimate goodness must be greater than any apparent manifestation of its opposite.

The result of affirmative prayer will always be a positive improvement, although it may not look like it initially. A friend of mine lamented her desire for a new car and the following week her car caught on fire. The result was a new car, but if she would have loaded up the fire experience with a lot of negative feelings and beliefs, she might have missed out on the greater good awaiting her, and the end result would have been diminished.

Demonstrations following affirmative prayer are like pouring liquid jello into a mold. We want the demonstration of solid jello or a specific form in an area of our life, but the speed of our demonstration is based on the Law of Logical and Sequential Evolution, i.e., liquid jello takes time to solidify. As Holmes described it, "There is no process of healing, but there is generally a process in healing. This process is the time and effort which we undergo in our realization of Truth." By trusting in the process without doubt, our demonstration unfolds perfectly. We know that conditions are not things. Conditions can be changed. The task is to reveal the truth and allow the Law to work harmoniously for our greater good.

Personal beliefs about right and wrong impact every aspect of life. Over time many values find their way into subjective or subconscious mind and from there they instinctively guide our actions and reactions. Feeling out of sync or in turmoil can often be traced to being out of integrity with our basic value system. Instead of letting this incongruity operate at the subconscious level, there is a benefit to periodically reassessing both our primary values and our value hierarchy. Values change over time and if our present behaviors don't match our values, it is time to modify one or the other to resolve the conflict. Periodically reflect on the highest values you hold. Do you know your top ten?

What are your values in the areas of relationships, commitments, love, and the health of your body? Does your life reflect living in integrity with those values? If not, consider changing your actions or changing your values to get back in integrity and regain inner harmony.

Wrong conditions could not exist if there wasn't someone to believe in them, so when a situation requires us to strengthen our faith, it helps to talk with someone like a Practitioner or Minister who can assist us in seeing life more clearly. The Practitioner knows that any apparent limiting condition cannot be supported by the Universe without the support of our beliefs. Our limitations have no power; we have the power. We use the Law without thinking most of the time. Through meditation and the daily use of affirmative prayer, our energy is focused on bringing more positive, loving, enjoyable experiences into life. It is not a use of willpower, but implementing our power of choice. This can be done by choosing power statements in affirmative prayers, expressing positive expectations, seeing our goal already in mind. Begin today.

DIALOGUE

I volunteered to help feed the homeless at a nearby shelter, but as I was serving food, I found myself judging those who came by as worthy or unworthy of my help. I can't seem to stop this judgment and see God in every person. How do I overcome this problem?

Sometimes when we do acts of kindness such as this, in the back of our mind we have an expectation about those who receive our gift. We expect they will be thankful, desire to change and will somehow see by our actions, there is a better way to live life. Again our expectations lead to our suffering. There is nothing we can do to control or change the minds of others, no matter how desperate they seem. What we can do is be a light of kindness, unconditional love, and non-judgment. When they are ready, they will seek the truth in their own way. This is the power of love, the gift we give by loving everyone, not the outer form, but loving the inner form, the divinity of God within. The next time your mind starts judging, turn to a spiritual practice, such as the repetition of the word "Namaste" (the Divine Spirit in me recognizes the Divine Spirit in you), seeing them from that place of love.

A person I work with is so negative, I try to be friendly to him every day, but I can't seem to get him to budge out of this pattern. Any ideas?

The truth is that we don't know the burdens other people carry. In my work as a Practitioner, many times I am amazed at the deep level of pain and suffering people carry around for years, yet I am so thankful for that moment when they reach out for healing, to move beyond the pain to experience greater peace and happiness. We cannot predict when that moment will happen. We cannot make it happen. What we can do is let go of our judgment, be fully present and clear about the power of love and Law. Know that spiritual evolution for ourselves and all of humanity is always upward.

AFFIRMATIVE PRAYER

GOD'S POWER IS UNLIMITED

Divine Mind is limitless. I recognize that there is only one power in the Universe and that is God. This power expresses as a sea of limitless opportunity for me to apply these principles in my life. In the big picture, in the true picture, there is never any conflict or confusion, because God is omnipotent. The knowledge of God's unlimited power, this Oneness with that power, envelopes me and protects me today.

As I allow this greater power to move through me and all of my affairs, I am engulfed in a great sense of peace. I am free of "having to do" and "having to be." God is. I am. We are One. In this knowing I recognize all of my friends and family as individualized expressions of God in action. We are all here to grow and learn in our own way in order to get in touch with our God-like nature. Whatever it looks like on the outside, there is only goodness, God-in-action, on the inside. I put this knowledge to use every day in my life, knowing how important it is for me to live in integrity. When I act out of love and caring for myself and others, all of my actions are right, because I act only in the spirit of love. I know what is best for me and, therefore, by the Law of Cause and Effect, what is right for me is also right for everyone in my environment. Whether they see it this way or not is insignificant. I know Law works each and every moment, because it is I who put Cause into action in my life. Right now I make love, not fear, the cause that rules my life. Living in love is the highest order. This inspires me to know more, be more, and experience more love, peace, and tranquility in my life.

My reality is that life moves upward and expands forever in the expression of my greater good. I can never lose my good, my life, or any person I love. We are all forever one in heart, mind and spirit, because we are one with God. I am so grateful for this knowing and I cooperate with it totally, without reservation. My life is a doorway through which love passes. I recognize it as Law and accept it as so. And so it is. Amen.

Lesson Five: Changing Race Consciousness

Much of the time the spiritual path is simply the expansion and maturing of our own perspective. Therefore, to understand race consciousness we must understand the soul. Soul is the subjective part of mind, our subconscious. As Ernest Holmes explained, "The Subjective Mind which we call Soul, is not a knower…It knows only to do without knowing why It does. It is a doer or executor of the will of the Spirit and has no choice of Its own." This is why co-creation is about working with the mind, since the mind is directly connected to Universal Mind, that part of the Universe, which existed before we did. Our beliefs in subjective mind are the cause of our experience, compared to objective mind, where we experience conscious individuality. Changing the beliefs embedded in subjective mind changes the effect of those beliefs and the form it takes in our life.

We are one with the rest of the world; our unity lies in subjective mind. With unity at that level, we are sensitive to the energy and thought vibrations of other people, places, and things. Subjective mind is intriguing because stored in its depths lies the memory of all people, places, things, and experiences that have ever occurred. It is one big history book from time immemorial. Subjective mind is where we also connect with the experiences of others and can pick up their thought patterns. Remember when you walked into a room of people and wanted to leave immediately? How about the time you entered a room and felt an overflowing sense of love and peace? These sensations are real. The atmosphere of any environment is shaped by our subjective mind and the minds of everyone there.

Evolution proceeds not by diluting the individual into the race, or even losing the individual in the cosmic ocean, but by fostering greater individuality through choice and initiative.

—Thomas Troward
The Creative Process of the Individual

In the depths of subjective mind resides an array of beliefs often called race consciousness. Ernest Holmes called it race suggestion and Thomas Troward called it race personality. Holmes felt we all have a tendency to recreate in our life the thread of beliefs that have accumulated over time. An example is the belief that we are not responsible for our experience and someone or something else is to blame (the government, our neighbor, our boss, etc.). Another race conscious belief is there is not enough to go around (money, fame, food, great men or great women, etc.). How about the world is a corrupt place; life is a struggle; it is rare to succeed in life; people will rip you off if you give them a chance. In most cases a race conscious belief is negative and deeply imbedded in our subconscious to the point where we don't realize its impact on our life. One way to change negative race conscious beliefs is to become aware of the beliefs we hold. This can be done through affirmative prayer, spiritual practices, contemplation, meditation, classes, reading spiritual texts, and discussions with practitioners of metaphysics. It is also the goal of affirmative prayer to neutralize the vibrations of our negative beliefs, replacing them with positive beliefs.

A phychic can enter the stream of thought of anyone whose vibration he can mentally contact, be that person in the flesh or out of it; and since we are all psychic—all having a soul element—we are all doubtless communicating with each other to the degree that we sympathetically vibrate toward each other.

—Ernest Holmes
The Science of Mind

Thomas Troward felt our personality as a human being developed from race personality. He believed evolution proceeds "not by diluting the individual into the race, but by fostering greater individuality through choice and initiative." By visualizing.

Troward's concept of evolution as an infinite upward spiral, individually we move forward whether we want to or not. We can go along with this easily or it can be very, very difficult. By deciding to learn and grow, we move up the ladder of evolution more gracefully. If instead we live with a mind dominated by negative race conscious beliefs, our ability to move forward in an understanding of truth is very limited. Do you recognize the race conscious beliefs you hold?

The vibration of our individual atmosphere is what generates the power of attraction between us and other people, places or things. When we meet someone who we instantly like, although we may not find their form attractive, this attraction comes from deep inside and bypasses our ego mind, which may prejudge a person as not worthy of our attention. Feelings and unspoken words are a very powerful guide in our relationship with others in the world.

Contemplate the number of communities in the world with starving or warring populations. Wouldn't it be wonderful if we could wave a big flag of truth and instantly people would become expressions of love instead of hate? Great teachers have said the population of a country cannot evolve with just a wave of a flag, because evolution on this path is a personal choice, it is done individually. When the consciousness of enough individuals is raised to a greater understanding and embodiment of truth, walls literally come tumbling down, as we witnessed in East Germany. It starts within each individual.

Subjective mind and race consciousness are the destination of affirmative prayer, which taps into Universal Mind where all things are known at all times. The goal of affirmative prayer is to change Cause, so we will experience its new and positive effects. Affirmative prayer plants seeds, like a farmer who plants corn in a fertile field. The inherent nature of the corn seed is to grow into a plant, and not just any plant—it grows into corn. The tiny seed contains within it the idea of a grown plant, and nature never contradicts the inherent ability of the seed to become a plant. The seed of our belief, which we call Cause, is set in motion by our belief (example: someone else is responsible for my problems), which when nurtured and watered, becomes a plant or experience in our life. It really looks like it, too! Affirmative prayer is a powerful tool for setting a new cause in motion that terminates the old negative belief.

> *Our further evolution is not into a state of less activity, but of greater; not into being less alive, but more alive; not into being less ourselves, but more ourselves—thus being just the opposite of those systems which present the goal of existence as reabsorption into the undifferentiated Divine essence.*
>
> —Thomas Troward
> The Creative Process of the Individual

The true clairvoyant taps into Universal Mind and can see the seed and the plant, even if the plant is not grown yet. Clairvoyants can see the unfolding of events in Universal mind because they tap into the continuation of unity, of being where there is no time. Cause and effect exist at every point, so if Cause has been put into motion, effect can be seen. But until the foreseen outcome occurs, it can be changed because the negative belief (Cause) can be changed. At any moment affirmative prayer can be used to change Cause, which will change the effect. This knowledge is the greatest gift metaphysics and the principles of co-creation offers to the world. You can use affirmative prayer to change those negative beliefs now. Start with the simple things. Proving affirmative prayer works is a powerful motivator to help us expand its use in all areas of life.

Subjective mind is a cooperator; it has no other choice, it always says "yes" and acts on our beliefs. This is the key to effective affirmative prayer work. An idea put into mind already has within it the power to express as effect, so Universal Mind knows how the idea or cause will be expressed. As Holmes wrote, "Every thought sets the fulfillment of its desire in motion in Mind, and Mind sees the thing as already done!"

A prophet has the ability to look at the subjective tendencies in Universal Mind, which have been stimulated by Cause, and see the outcome before it actually manifests. This is like watching two trains speeding down the same railroad tracks towards each other. If we stand on a hill observing the trains, we see the anticipated result—the prophecy would be a crash. The prophet taps into subjective mind and through logical deduction, sees the tendency towards completion. Affirmative prayer removes a negative seed (the oncoming crash) and plants a positive one (a different track or a malfunction that makes the trains stop). There are an infinite number of ways to avoid the crash. Spiritual practices tap into Universal Mind, and by using affirmative prayer to change a core belief, the effect is changed and the outcome shifts.

> *We are who we are as much because of our gaps and failures as because of our strengths.*
>
> —Thomas Moore
> Care of the Soul

One way to reveal race conscious beliefs and our dominant core beliefs is through meditation. Many of these beliefs were placed into subjective mind throughout time, by our environment, experiences, and those who had authority over us. But we always have dominion over our life. We can take conscious control and tell subjective mind what we wish to experience. In order to differentiate whether an idea has come from a deeply held race conscious belief, ask these questions: Does the belief express more life? Does it expand our good for the self and those around us? Does it express love? If it is in alignment with love, life, and unity, it must be in harmony with Universal Spirit. Those core beliefs will serve us, as well as everyone in our environment.

Death is a deeply embedded race conscious belief, an accepted outcome of our life in this form. It is one of those beliefs that is so ingrained, it is often difficult to differentiate whether it is a universal law or a belief. History has shown that Jesus and others have overcome this consciousness and resurrected. Thomas Troward calls this "entering the Fifth Kingdom," a place where we are fully aware of our Divinity. In the Fifth Kingdom he says we recognize our body as simply substance, entirely responsive to our will. Troward concluded that eternal life in an immortal, physical body is the logical outcome of evolution. But few people throughout history have attained this level of realization. Therefore, the generally held belief is that we must pass through the transition called death.

Our ability to change race conscious beliefs can be improved by being aware of the pictures, images, and symbols brought into conscious mind by our intuitive, subjective mind. Intuition is that inner knowing, that gut feeling of right and wrong, which always tries to keep objective mind informed. Often we are too busy to recognize the importance of intuitive thought because intuition is not always logical, but it is generally correct.

We can develop our intuition in a variety of ways, such as using affirmations, focusing techniques, imagery, inner peace through meditation, contemplation, journaling, and physical exercise. When an intuitive feeling arises and that gut feeling appears, take a moment and bring it into conscious mind. If the feeling persists, go with it. This was brought home to me recently when intuition led me to stop and get gas for my car at a station with a long waiting line. I found myself pulling in line before I consciously recognized that this is something I don't do. As I sat waiting, wondering what this was all about, I heard a frantic woman on the pay phone. Her car had broken down on the way to pick up her young son. Without thinking, I asked her if I could help. In a flash I was pulling my car out of line, taking the grateful woman to retrieve her son. All I could do was smile and give thanks to Spirit that I was awake enough to let intuition be my guide.

Every little thing is sent for something, and in that thing there should be happiness and the power to make happy. Like the grasses showing tender faces to each other, thus we should do, for this was the wish of the Grandfathers of the World.

—Black Elk
Black Elk Speaks

Plotinus tells us there are three ways by which we gather knowledge: through science, through opinion, and through intuition. Holmes complements this by saying, "Intuition is Spirit knowing Itself." Intuitive channels represent spiritual capacities; each is an avenue leading to self-knowingness. As we expand our awareness of intuitive thought, we can use it to identify race conscious beliefs. Over time intuition can help us clarify and strengthen our skill, until we reach a point where we just know the truth.

Another popular race conscious belief is the acceptance of violence as a natural part of being human. The belief in violence is almost as deeply ingrained in our subconscious as the belief in death. At first conscious mind says this cannot be true, but upon reflection we see how the belief in violence permeates society and the world. Television shows promote violence as part of life, like the old phrase, "Truth, justice, and the American way." But to shift our consciousness to a belief in non-violence requires that we continually weed out violent thoughts (even the smallest provoking thoughts) and replace them with love. This is a daunting task. One cannot just announce non-violence on a loud speaker and expect it to happen. Recognize that when we feel the smallest bit of anger, it is the seed for violence.

A Buddhist monk, Thich Nhat Hanh, writes, teaches, and practices non-violence. Growing up in Vietnam, he personally walked the difficult path during the war, trying to shift both the Vietnamese and American governments away from their commitment to violent action. In reading his book, "Love In Action," the numerous monks who followed this path in their quest for non-violence, can be great modern examples. Much like the crucifixion and suffering of Jesus, the monks were willing to accept great suffering in order to awaken others. Speaking out for non-violence, they were condemned at the time as pro-communist neutralists. Thich Nhat Hanh believes "a government is only a reflection of society, which is a reflection of our own consciousness. To create fundamental change, we, the members of society, have to transform ourselves. If we want real peace, we have to demonstrate love and understanding personally so that those responsible for making decisions can learn from us." Going to the essence of the problem, he sees blame, anger, and arguing as forms of violence. Should we just stand back and avoid violence? He explains the difference between non-violence and non-action, "When we see social injustice, if we practice non-action, we may cause harm. When people need us to say or do something, if we don't, we can kill by our inaction or our silence."

> *There is a time in every man's education when he arrives at the conviction that envy is ignorance; that imitation is suicide; that he must take himself for better for worse as his portion; that though the wide universe is full of good, no kernel of nourishing corn can come to him but through his toil bestowed on that plot of ground which is given to him to till.*
>
> —Ralph Waldo Emerson
> Essay on Self Reliance

Again, let's reflect on the soul. Subjective mind, the soul, knows only to do without knowing why. It is the doer. This is why metaphysics and affirmative prayer are so powerful. Affirmative prayer works with our mind, which is directly connected to Universal Mind. Our deeply held beliefs, positive and negative, are the cause of our experience. Let the power of affirmative prayer, combined with your belief in love and goodness, replace any ingrained negative beliefs so that your life may more profoundly express those same qualities. Begin today.

DIALOGUE

You have mentioned the value of meditation, but I don't know how to do it. Can you explain meditation in more detail?

In simple terms, meditation is the stilling of the mind, which is most easily done in a quiet place in your home. I have a corner in my bedroom where I have placed spiritual reminders, things that help bring me to that still place within. The phrase I think best fits the description of meditation is finding the space between our thoughts. As we enlarge that space, the place where there is no thinking, we strengthen our connection with Universal Mind. Although sitting in quiet meditation is calming and cleansing, meditation is an active tool through which clear intuitive thoughts can come to the conscious mind. You may hear people say that they came to a decision by meditating on an issue or question. They sit down, and before silencing the mind, they focus on the question they want answered. In the silence we can receive guidance and answers to questions from the soul level. To do this requires letting all thoughts just float by, even though the ego mind wants to grab one and focus on it.

Meditation is a powerful tool and it is as Holmes said, "Do not just sit by and hope something will happen. A passive meditation will never produce an active demonstration..." To work out our problems, Holmes advised taking "daily take time to meditate and mentally treat the condition, no matter what the apparent contradictions may be." He explains, in this way we are working silently in the Law and the Law will find an outlet through our faith in it.

AFFIRMATIVE PRAYER

THIS IS MY MOMENT

God is all there is. This presence is the only power that exists. It is the power of pure, pure love. I recognize that I have been created as an individualized expression of that One Power, therefore, the essence of my being is love. This is the moment when I claim love, which is God, as the One and Only Power in my life. Deep within my soul is where unconditional love and wisdom reside; they are the essence of my being.

As I focus my consciousness on my oneness with God, I accept this clear knowing with all my heart. Every action I take further reveals this truth. This moment is one of active creation as I tap the energy of my soul and, through focused thought, walk easily in my journey to the light. It is clear to me now the power I release by welcoming enriching relationships, unlimited energy and vitality, and total success into and as my life experience. Through my connection with Universal Mind, through God, all things are possible.

I realize that God's Mind and my mind are one. Knowing that I have been led to this moment, I give thanks for all the experiences that brought me to this place. I am awake; I am aware. I consciously turn within to hear the inner wisdom and allow it to guide me. Every day is an opportunity to experience an expanded awareness of my God-self.

My mind is filled with joyous expectations, for I know that I am a spiritual being. I am thankful to know these words are true. I celebrate the Law of Mind by thinking clear and positive thoughts that create a wonderful life. And so it is. Amen.

Lesson Six: Unity and Individuality

Are you comforted to know that enlightenment is an ongoing process? It is true, we never reach a place where our development stops; we are eternally evolving. But since we also know that God is all there is, in what way do we relate this to all of life's ups and downs? I think Ken Wilbur said it beautifully, "And so forms continue to arise, and you learn to surf."

Surfing is such a wild and exhilarating sport that requires intense concentration on the motion of the water and becoming one with it. Hard and fast, up and down, small and great, the waves of the ocean keep coming, just like life experiences. A surfer practices and develops strength and skills to work in harmony with the unpredictable nature of the ocean. Maintaining that sense of oneness takes focused effort and determination. With awareness and practice we, too, can hone our spiritual skills and surf harmoniously through life.

> *The Infinite never expresses itself in fragments. There is no such a thing as a part of God. In an indivisible unity, all of everything is present everywhere all the time.*
>
> —Ernest Holmes
> The Anatomy of Healing Prayer

Inner peace and harmony comes from living in the knowledge of our oneness with God and all things. But there are times when we become hypnotized by our earthly experiences. We might inflate our own importance a little too much and it can be difficult to feel and see the unity around us. When we feel separate, our mind can be dominated by selfish urges, putting forth effort to have their own way to do only what we like, while we are unable to see at that moment, how we might help those around us. Jesus taught that we should not wait for a negative experience (a crash) to let go of our attachment to separateness, but to consciously turn away from those selfish needs and do something positive. By turning away from the darkness of separateness we walk into the light.

Light accompanies an expansion of consciousness. When we connect with our soul in deep meditation, we can see white light. If it could be seen with open eyes, affirmative prayer would be seen as a pathway of light. Holmes said, "This light is not created. It is not a psychological explosion; it is something which pre-exists." And in this illumination something is felt.

One way to see how perfectly both unity and individuality express in life is to observe rain. Eventually rainwater always returns to the ocean. Water may pause here or there in a lake or stream; it may evaporate into the clouds or be taken up by a thirsty plant; it may be the ice cubes that keep a glass of water cool. While water experiences its many forms, the ocean does not worry or fret—it just is. It waits patiently, knowing every drop of water is not lost, it is just on a journey of individual expression and will eventually find its way back into a stream, which eventually joins in perfect union with the ocean. All spiritual teachers have said we also eventually find our way back to a true recognition of oneness, our true nature. It may take some people longer than others—pausing as long as water frozen in a glacier—but at some point each one melts and finds their way back home.

Einstein expressed unity in his recognition of energy and mass being equal, identical, and interchangeable. The basis for metaphysics is the concept that there is no difference between the thought and what it does; there is no difference between the thought and the form it takes. How could thought change a form unless form were thought as form? It just couldn't. That is the whole basis of affirmative prayer. Just as an acorn becomes a tree, a solid thought creates the thing. How? Nobody knows, and it doesn't matter. What matters is that it happens. Holmes explains, "Then our aim is not to speak the right word, necessarily, but a word that is so completely accepted that it can operate." Do you remember a moment when you made a personal decision and it was so clear nothing was going to stop you? Determination and clarity are very powerful partners.

> *In the ultimate depths of your own awareness, you intersect infinity.*
>
> —Ken Wilber
> A Brief History of Everything

Dr. Raymond Charles Barker points this out in his book, *The Power of Decision.* He writes, "The universe is undisturbed by human stupidity and ignorance of what the individual really can be. The universe is never in a hurry. It is law and order. It waits for the individual to come to his senses and know himself aright. Once you know yourself as Mind, you forevermore control your experience through ideas, and not through the manipulation of material events." So are you ready? Where on your spiritual path have you been resting in eddies? Can you think of one small decision today that will move you forward? Knowing that the universe is behind you 100% and will support your decision to the degree you are clear and determined, what is one step you can take today towards what you want the most? Let affirmative prayer support this decision daily and watch the perfection unfold. It is the Law and it works.

When we are with friends and feel unity with the world, there is a sense of lightness in our body. Problems and worries fade into the distance. We intuitively know there is more to this life experience, it allows feelings of separateness to wash away. Scientists understand unity, because science has shown there is no energy that will destroy itself. We are dealing with One Mind, One Spirit, which expresses through thought, just as the thought of God expresses as all. Knowing how the Law of the Universe works, we can now focus on our thoughts while being consciously aware of the words we speak, because they will mold our life experience. Working with Law, we can now prove to ourselves that Law exists, so we thoroughly understand that our state of consciousness is in continuous creation.

"The great, the good, and the wise" have told us this 'thing,' this Divine essence is light, life, love, peace, power, beauty, and joy; divine attributes we can observe around us every day of the week. Troward describes these as attributes of Spirit, and as we contemplate each one, we become it. Spirit holds the possibility of everything and it resides in our individual consciousness. This Divine Mind is the field in which we plant our seeds; it is the field of eternal action. In each thing the Presence of God must exist as the idea and the potentiality of that thing in which it is incarnated. The potentiality of a tomato plant resides in the seed. How the seed received this identity is the process of evolution. "Within us must be the potential of everything we shall ever evolve into," writes Holmes. Just think of what has evolved over this past hundred years as a new century begins—computers, atomic war, airplanes, telephones, space stations…All of these things had the potential to exist many centuries ago—the potential was there, but it was the evolution of our thinking process, our knowledge and understanding, that put the pieces together to create a laptop computer.

> *Duplicity is a lie, the fundamental lie, the original untruthfulness—and the beginning of the 'small self,' the battered self, the self that hides its Original Face in the forms of its own suffering.*
>
> —Ken Wilber
> A Brief History of Everything

Evolution is a PRINCIPLE, which manifests in all form. It is the effect of Intelligence, not its cause. Evolution, the effect, only follows Involution, the idea. When we embody the idea, the form appears, which is why we believe behind everything is the movement of consciousness. Every idea we have is God expressing the Self. It is God's nature to know and crave expression. Every aspect of our life is Cause and Effect in action. Spirit Involves and Law Evolves mechanically. Evolution is an effect. Take a moment to look at your life and find the connection between: Involution...Evolution; Thought...Thing; Word...Law; Purpose...Execution.

Many sacred scriptures throughout the ages have taught unity and individuality. One text that focuses on spiritual self-mastery is the *Bhagavad Gita*. The epic stories found here are metaphors for the war between the forces of light and darkness in every person; the war between unity and individuality. In Chapter 2 of the text, spiritual teacher, Sri Krishna, reminds his student, Arjuna, of his immortal nature, the real Self that never dies, the eternal Self. The basic premise as Arjuna begins his path of spiritual awareness, is that the immortal soul is more important than the passing world. But Arjuna is told he will not fully realize this until he can see beyond the dualities of life and identify with the immortal Self through direct mystical experience. Krishna calls for disciplining the mind and detachment from dualities like pain and pleasure. The goal of the story is to teach that by expanding our spiritual awareness, our reaction to events will not be based on habit, but will be based on the freedom of non-attachment. Here again we find the power of the witness consciousness.

Krishna goes on to talk to Arjuna about attachment. "When you keep thinking about sense objects, attachment comes. Attachment can breed desire, the lust of possession that turns to anger. Anger clouds the judgment; you can no longer learn from past mistakes. Lost is the power to choose between what is wise and what is unwise; and your life is utter waste. But when you move amidst the world of sense, free from attachment and aversion alike, there comes the peace in which all sorrows end, and you live in the wisdom of the Self." When we enter this state of awareness, we feel bliss, then soon we again become aware of our body, our physical experience, and the sense of unity may fade like a dream. The moment we pierce the veil of illusion and touch infinity, our life changes. Consistent spiritual practices are the path to keep this channel of deep inner understanding open.

Spiritual wisdom starts the day that we know from now on every discovery is either a discovery of the self or related to the self in the Cosmic Mind. The self must raise the self by the self.

—Ernest Holmes
The Anatomy of Healing Prayer

Heaven and hell are states of consciousness. We choose the degree to which we experience heaven or hell, because suffering is a conscious choice. Ernest Holmes believed that someday we will have learned all we need to through suffering and will decide that we've had enough. He believed we will reach this point through an evolutionary process and expressed it this way: "Evolution is the awakening of the soul to a recognition of its unity with the Whole." We will evolve into infinity. Behind evolution is an irresistible pressure compelling us to be more, better, higher, greater. We shall make progress, expanding in a sequence from where we are to whatever we shall become, forever spiraling upward. Evolution is what Troward and Holmes both believed begins with involution, where Spirit becomes matter, where we go within to become a conscious co-creator with God, which then evolves into higher and higher degrees of consciousness. Evolution is the process of Matter becoming Spirit—going back to our Oneness.

Mystics helped us to know that we, too, could reveal the Presence of God and have a deep spiritual perception. They didn't read our thoughts, but sensed the atmosphere of God. In our escalating abilities, we can hear and read about God, but the best knowledge is direct experience. The best method is to learn it for ourselves, not second hand. What we experience is all we can know. Mother Teresa had a great gift of experiencing Jesus in everyone. She would say, "Each one is Jesus in His distressing disguise." How blissful that vision must be.

Conscious evolution progresses with things as simple as letting go of a belief in duality and recognizing that right and left, up and down, are just two sides of the same coin. The speed of our upward movement depends on how fast we let go of the negative beliefs we have carried around for a long time, such as blame or judgment. As we choose to be in a witness consciousness, where we are the observer, we see beyond labels of good and bad, inside and out, and know the truth about any situation. The freedom of sensing unity with everything makes it easier to let go of habits and patterns that don't serve us. Then we can trust in Spirit, let go of negativity knowing the Universe abhors a vacuum and will always fill it. The goal is to let go of the negative, be the observer, and know the Universe will fill us with love. Again, by letting go, our old habits will die from lack of attention.

> *The only knowledge we have of the kingdom of God or of heaven must come through the consciousness of man. The mind should swing between meditation and action.*
>
> —Evelyn Underhill
> English religious writer

By letting go, does this mean we won't have any more temptations? No. Like Ram Dass says, our ingrained habits never totally go away, but instead come back to us periodically like little schmoozes that tickle us, saying, "Are you really done with this one?" It makes me laugh, because when that happens I can really see how far I've progressed on letting go of that one! To me it's the ultimate cosmic giggle.

Getting into a witness consciousness in times of stress can be a challenging, but it is such a powerful tool. It offers us the optional perspective to think, "So this is my challenge," instead of getting drawn into the drama and negativity of a situation. When we are in that clear space, we can see the play of consciousness in the participants and then we can positively contribute to the situation with love. When we look at the ocean as a witness, that moment of pause gives us the feeling of oneness with the purity of the ocean, its rhythm and power, and the purity of our self. The sensation of being in the witness consciousness and the sensation we have when observing the ocean are the same. Unity is when we feel two sides of one experience, one reality. But so often we are not the witness and we don't feel Oneness. It is not that Oneness comes and goes, it is our understanding that comes and goes.

Oneness just is. There has never been one second in all time when Oneness did not exist.

One of the shifts in my consciousness, after growing up Catholic and then finding metaphysics, was in discovering that Jesus was a mystic. There have been many mystics throughout the ages and they all agree that the soul is the pathway of self-discovery, where we find unity in all aspects of life. The great mystics like Jesus, Moses, Buddha, Mohammed, all talked with God and came to know God as "personal to those who believe in It's presence." They felt it is natural for us to turn to the Great Power behind everything. When we sincerely turn to God, not just in a time of need, we should get the sense of a Real Presence. In metaphysics we do this by turning within to find that place of inner peace and the recognition of God as our reality. Begin today.

DIALOGUE

My daughter is very distraught with her work and life and doesn't know what to do. She won't listen to me, so how can I help?

The most important thing to do is realize that your daughter has within her the knowledge and ability to solve her problems. Fear may be holding her back, but fear has no foundation in truth. Within her is the answer. The first action to take is to do affirmative prayer for this purpose: my daughter has all of the knowledge of the Universe at her disposal. She is capable of making any changes in her life that are needed. She is totally supported by the Universe in her decisions, because it is the nature of the Universe to support her beliefs. Nothing holds her back; she has been experiencing life as she believed it to be. Know that she now sees the truth behind any experience and in confidence can go forward and bring into her experience a job filled with joy and satisfaction. Her dreams are fulfilled. I suggest you just share the essence of your prayer with her so she knows you care, but are not making decisions for her. This will help empower her to do what she knows in her heart is right.

Sometimes I think about all of the poor countries, wars, starving people and I feel so sad and helpless. I want to help, but I fear I could be consumed by the magnitude of the problem. This is a dilemma!

I know this feeling, and every time it comes up I go back to the Source. All of humanity is evolving at their level of acceptance. When I look at the consciousness of various communities of people around the world, it can be very sad. I can say in total confidence that those people who are starving and warring also are on their own spiritual path. They are Spirit in action, evolving at their own pace, in their own way. Here we are at this level of knowledge and experience, which doesn't mean we are better than…but we can be lights of awareness, to show a new way of living life as a human being. We are beings of light for others looking for the answer. Our job is to do what we can within reasonable bounds, which we determine, but to also be the light…to live our life as an example. We don't have to preach or lecture, just be the best we can be. This is our gift every moment. Give more of your gift today!

AFFIRMATIVE PRAYER

PERFECT PRAYER IS MY DIVINE NATURE

There is only one power and presence in this life. It is the ever-present energy of God, of Spirit, showing Itself in its many forms. I recognize that God expresses through each and every thing I see, including myself. I am a divine expression of that power, living life as only I know how.

No matter what happens, I am aware of Spirit guiding and directing my way. I see a divine Intelligence at work within every situation, every person. Each day my experience gives me an opportunity to awaken in a greater way to who and what I truly am. Today I know for those I meet, that they, too, are unique and divine beings. All of us are on our individual pathway of life. Our interactions are the gift we both give and receive, a learning experience, and an opportunity to reveal the Presence of God.

I embrace each person, each challenge, each occurrence, and I understand how it serves me. There is only God fully expressing in all. I surrender any and all reservations about whether others are supported by the Universe. My experience tells me—I feel it, I taste it, I know it, hear it and see it; God is all there is.

In great thanksgiving I release any worry or concern for those I meet. I give what I can when I can. My compassion for others is like a light that shines for others to see, to receive just as I receive, the experience of the power and the presence of God. There are no accidents. My life unfolds in the gratitude and beauty I hold in my heart. I feel honored to be a part, even if it is a small part, of the lives of so many beautiful souls, all on their individual paths. Thank you, God. I release my concerns to your greater wisdom and love. And so it is. Amen.

Lesson Seven: Metaphysics, Physics, and the Changeless

By this time I hope you have felt the inner peace that comes from knowing your Oneness with God and all things. With it, you have also understood what we physically touch and see are not as they appear, but that all of life is infinitely more fascinating! In just observing the things in life, it is easy to feel separate from our true spiritual nature, but when we take time to touch that place of deep inner peace and feel the powerful Presence of Spirit, there is such comfort in knowing we are never alone.

In this chapter we look at the relationship of metaphysics to physics. The study of physics includes matter and energy, the study of physical processes and properties of a system, such as the transpiration of water through plants or the strength properties of steel. Metaphysics, on the other hand, is the study of what lies beyond the physical and, according to Webster, is concerned with the fundamental nature of reality, what lies outside our objective experience. Metaphysics includes the physical and more—it includes that part of the physical and fundamental nature of reality that is changeless.

Eminent physicist, Albert Einstein, wrote, "The whole of science is nothing more than a refinement of everyday thinking." Sounds a little bit like race consciousness. He felt strongly that our common community experience is derived through our senses, our interpretation of pictures, images, and feelings which appear stronger and more fixed in our community than our individual experience. Scientists work to find connections and relationships that we can comprehend through our senses, as Einstein explained, "to establish general rules which determine the reciprocal connection of objects and events in time and space." These connections become a ridged set of rules used by scientists to explain how something works. Yet connections beyond the physical, such as intuition or prayer, do not adapt well to these fixed rules.

Science without religion is lame, religion without science is blind.

—Albert Einstein
Ideas and Opinions

At one point in our history, scientific opinion held that beliefs should be replaced by knowledge, because beliefs not based on scientific knowledge were just superstition. Einstein felt that scientific methods are not the only way to explore our world, and wrote, "The scientific method can teach us nothing else beyond how facts are related to, and conditioned by, each other." Looking at the major religions of his time, Einstein felt that the future of religion should not be focused on living in fear of God, but in gaining rational knowledge about our spiritual nature. This is the gift of studying metaphysics.

The focal point of metaphysics is Spirit, the life force, the vital energy, the source of life apart from our physical body. Spirit is at the center and circumference of everything, visible and not visible. It has no opposites, no opposition, no enemies, no separation. Spirit is love, creativity, and harmony. Spirit is Cause and Effect. In our life, Spirit is the "medium of thought, power and action."

In the previous chapter we reviewed evolution as a constant. As Holmes said, "Creation is the passing of Spirit into form and is eternally going on.... The Spirit is conscious of Its own Thought, Its own Desire, Its own manifest Action; and It is conscious that Its Desire is satisfied. Consequently, It is conscious of that which It manifests; but It is not conscious of any effort or process in Its manifestation." It just is. This is what is meant in metaphysics when we say Law is impersonal. Law does not know Itself; Law only knows to do. This is how Spirit operates, It creates by contemplation.

Fascinating, isn't it, to realize that by our thought we tap into Spirit, who only knows "to do," to react to our thought by creating every moment, which is why we call it Law. How was Law made? To our knowledge, Law has always been. Could there be a time when Law did not operate? It seems impossible because of the ongoing creative nature of the Universe. Continuing evolution is co-existent with God and therefore must be co-eternal with Spirit. All action must be Spirit operating as Law.

> *The Body of the Universe is the result of the thought of Spirit, operating through the medium of Soul.*
>
> —Ernest Holmes
> The Science of Mind

By looking at how all of this works together, we touch a deeper understanding of the concept of the Trinity. In many religions we find the Trinity expressed as The Father, The Son, and The Holy Ghost.

In metaphysics we see the power of the Trinity expressed in several ways, such as:

THE TRIUNE NATURE OF THE ONE GOD

God & Law	Spirit & Creation	Substance into Form
	*******************************	
Spirit	Soul	Body
	*******************************	
Absolute Intelligence	Receptive Intelligence	Divine Ideas
	*******************************	
Intelligence	Substance	Form
	*******************************	
Cause	Medium	Effect
	*******************************	

To apply the basic laws of metaphysics in our life, recognize there are two simple principles at its core, which cannot be physically grasped; one is the power of love. We have not physically touched love as it moves from one person to another, but we do see the results of love. Think for a moment about the last time someone wrapped their arms around you and said, "I love you." The warmth and joy of being loved is an inside job. The glow that emanates from being loved is how we see principle at work.

> *There is no such thing as your mind, my mind and God's Mind. There is only Mind, in which we all live and move and have our being.*
>
> —Ernest Holmes
> The Science of Mind

The first core principle of metaphysics is: The Universe is Absolute Intelligence. This Intelligence is Self-Existent; It has always existed. Spirit was not created. This reminds me of a childhood recitation that now seems more profound in its meaning: 'God always was, always will be, and always will remain the same.' One physicist quoted by Einstein, viewed the Universe as "an Infinite Thinker, thinking mathematically." The Infinite Thinker being Absolute Intelligence, God/Spirit, while the math is Law, the process of Cause and Effect.

Belief + Law = Manifestation

The second principle of metaphysics is: Life is a process of Cause and Effect, which we choose to use positively or negatively. The effects in our life can be changed because Cause, the belief that began the chain reaction, can be changed. Holmes believed not only what is set in motion can be changed, but when the Truth is known it is demonstrated. This is why thoughts and beliefs are so powerful. When we create negative experiences, it may be difficult to accept that the experience came from a deeply held belief, consciously or unconsciously. Our beliefs are like a magnet drawing people, places, things, and experiences that support our belief. Sometimes a person comes into our life for no apparent reason. They are there and we don't know why, but through our association with them something in us changes. Possibly something inside us grows or expands, or something negative is released that had no other way to be released.

Looking back in time we can all recognize a person who came and went in our life that changed us in some way, and our appreciation of life expanded. No one comes into our experience by accident, but we achieve a great leap in understanding when we recognize that every detail of our personal life and our environment is a reflection of our beliefs. Since everything is Spirit in Action, seen and unseen, the logical conclusion is that Law always unfolds perfectly. If we don't like what we are experiencing, we can change it, for the power resides in us.

At the same time, if there is no challenge in life, there is no opportunity for spiritual growth.

> *No one has seen God at any time. If we love one another, God abides in us. By this we know that we abide in Him and He in us, because He has given us of His Spirit.*
>
> —1 John 4:12–13

We could make ourselves paranoid by thinking every word we utter will result in a demonstration. If that was the case, our chattering mind would create pure chaos and the world would certainly self-destruct. It is the degree to which we have embodied the idea or thought that stimulates the creative power. Recognize we are dealing with a mechanical process. At the same time, behind this process is the pure love of Infinite Intelligence. We can waste a lot of time wishing that the love of God would occasionally change Law, but the mechanical process of Law is consistent. It won't say "Oh, you really don't deserve that bad experience, I'll give you something better." If we jump off a building, Law will not change its mind and push us upward—we will fall down. Gravity works the same for everyone. In the pursuit of our spiritual awakening, it is important to understand that which is changeless. We connect with this place in meditation. Whenever we return to that space between our thoughts, we tap into the changeless. The love of God for all creation never changes; it is a love that permeates the Universe and supports our choice every time. God says "YES" whether our beliefs expand or limit us.

The essence of God is much more than just a mechanical process, it is a process based in love. Behind the mechanical nature is an energy constantly pushing us forward and supporting us in a greater expression of life. Thomas Troward explained life is an ever expanding, upward spiral. At the base of our personality, and every personality, is love, an inherent part of Universal energy. Love dissolves all fear; love is the light that dissipates the darkness and removes the shadows. It is the most powerful presence in the Universe, because it is the essence of

God. As individual creations of God, our personalization of Spirit must be personal to God. There is an individual level of intimacy between each one of us and Spirit. We are unfolding in harmony with the pulse of the Universe. It is comforting to know that no matter what path of learning we take, we are always being cradled in the loving arms of God. We are a spirit while God is The Spirit. We are an individual, while God is the Universal. We are a little world within ourselves, but we are not limited because we are merged with Universal Spirit. We are really One with God; we share the same essence in different degrees. We are a little circle within the big circle.

> *Our depressions, jealousies, narcissism, and failures are not at odds with the spiritual life. Indeed, they are essential to it. When tended, they prevent the spirit from zooming off into the ozone of perfectionism and spiritual pride.*
>
> —Thomas Moore
> Care of The Soul

There are many ways to connect with Universal Spirit and see the beauty of our little circle and its natural place in the big circle, but the materialistic tendencies of society do not help us in this respect. Thomas Moore describes this in his book, *Care of The Soul,* "In the late 1400's Ficino wrote in his *Book of Life* that spirit and body, religion and world, spirituality and materialism can all be trapped in a polarizing split: the more compulsively materialist we are, the more neurotic our spirituality will be, and vice versa." Moore goes on to explain how we can cure materialism by finding concrete ways to put soul back into our spiritual practices, our intellectual life, and our emotional and physical activities with the world.

When we do not feel the essence of our soul, it is easy to let the narrow viewpoints of others overshadow the richness of life. We can find ourselves taking a more fundamentalist approach that ignores personal choice and responsibility in favor of a more structured path. As Moore explains, "The tragedy of fundamentalism in any context is its capacity to freeze life into a solid cube of meaning." How often do we do that? How often do we ignore the mystery of the soul and instead, force our beliefs into a square package with colorful wrapping paper and a bow so it is simple, easy, and makes others feel comfortable? While our mind may crave meaning, structure, and complete answers, our soul craves depth, and delights in the time we spend on reflection, mindlessness, and daydreaming.

Yet life is never without some shadow. How would we appreciate beauty or joy if we could not compare a good experience with a not-so-good experience? In our busy day-to-day world it is easy to ignore spiritual practices, contact with our soul, in favor of joining in the rush of life or personal or materialistic pleasures. In my experience the shadows of our mind surface to refocus our attention. At first there comes a feather, a soft touch that may tickle us into awareness. But if we ignore the feather, then subconscious mind tosses a pebble, which makes us a little uncomfortable, but it may not be enough to awaken us to reconnect with our soul, our path, our purpose in life. If the pebble doesn't work, next a rock hurtles towards us, which hurts and challenges us to stop-look-listen. But with such a busy life, it is easy to dismiss the bruise and assume the rock wasn't really meant for us. Then comes a boulder, a major negative experience jarring us to the foundation of our being. This experience could be serious health problems or personal trauma. How many warnings have we ignored? Is there an area in your life where you are ignoring a feather or a pebble?

> *We should walk in newness of life by attracting, building up, enlightening and lighting up our neighbor, as John says: 'he was the light of men. This is the consciousness of compassion, seeing God everywhere.*
>
> —Meister Eckhart
> Meister Eckhart, From Whom God Hid Nothing

Meister Eckhart (1260–1357), a Dominican friar, preacher, author, and spiritual counselor, focused his work on a branch of theology concerned with the ultimate destiny of humankind, while recognizing that eternal life begins in the present moment. His writings contain a profound, yet simple guideline, called the Fourfold Path of Creation Spiritual Experience. An abbreviated version is: Path 1—Know the essence, virtue, and power of God is in all things. Path 2—Let go of all preconceptions and hold a deep reverence for all things. Path 3—Be aware and use the silence to let God speak and work through us. Path 4—Live in the consciousness of compassion in every situation by seeing God there. We are in this life experience; we cannot pretend we are not. There are responsibilities with this life that require effort, which can be made easier and more blissful by consciously embodying the principles of metaphysics and using a guide like Eckhart's Fourfold Path. Whether we accept the presence of God in all or refuse to take responsibility for our choices in life, we cannot avoid the consequences.

Every moment is a choice and we can choose to soar like an eagle, using one wing of grace, our personal connection with Spirit, and one wing of personal effort. Connect with the harmony, joy, peace, and love of God expressing as you, expressing both unity and individuality. Begin today.

DIALOGUE

I work in a very busy professional office where there are short deadlines and usually the air is full of tension. People are very quick to judge one another if there is any hint that we are not constantly giving our best. If this is a reflection of my beliefs, how can I change this situation?

The office environment is a great place to watch the interaction of every person's beliefs on display and interfacing with everyone else's beliefs, which in this instance creates the atmosphere you describe as tension. By identifying what in us contributes to that atmosphere, such as doubt, judgment, second-guessing our work, feeling less qualified or not equal to others, we can pinpoint our Cause for having that experience. When we change Cause, everything in our experience will change—everything. A change in Cause will change our effect and thus change the experience of everyone around us.

Prove this to yourself. Put yourself into a state of love and peace before going into a meeting and stay in that space. You can shift the consciousness of everyone in the room just by your approach, seeing the presence of God in all. There is no need for drama or tension when you put the pure power of love into action.

AFFIRMATIV PRAYER

I AM FREE

There is only One, One Power, One Presence, and that is God. This power is the Source, the Cause of all that I see, feel, touch, and know. This power is a Universal presence that resounds with boundless energy, moving outward, upward, with total freedom just to be. Freedom is God in action, to create and manifest as me.

From this day forward nothing holds me back from life. I free myself from doubt or worry. I let go of judgment and criticism. I focus on the Truth of my being; I am a unique individual expression of the One. I am an infinite and eternal being. Every activity in my life is Divine!

In this moment I recognize every form is God in full expression and in this recognition I stand in awe of all creation, the sun, the moon, the stars, and even the tiniest flower in bloom. The strength I receive from this realization is used to find the perfect outlet to fulfill my potential by becoming more than I ever thought possible. A greater good is available to me now; it is a part of my divine heritage. I become more, achieve more, experience more, because I am more than I previously imagined. It is the nature of everything in the Universe to expand outward, upward, forever.

Understanding this Truth about life sets me free today. I show my appreciation for this gift by using my time wisely and for the greater good of all in my life. I move into my infinite potential effortlessly and easily, letting go of anything that would distract me from blossoming fully. I am free. I am divine. And so it is. Amen.

Lesson Eight: Demonstrating Success and Happiness

The search for success and happiness can be an endless quest, if we assume just having money or things is the goal, yet sometimes it does feel like if we only had that special something, life would be much better. We know that achieving happiness through the accumulation of things is an illusion, but this does not stop us from dreaming. The good news is that all successful and happy experiences begin with ideas, with dreams of how our life could really be.

In studying metaphysics, we find there is a process, a way of handling these thoughts and feelings to get the best out of life. Ironically the most powerful way to accomplish this is to give the best of ourselves to every endeavor. We cannot receive what we cannot give—it is a law of reciprocal action. Remember the feather, the pebble, and the rock are ways Spirit gives us progressively noticeable indicators to pay attention and shift something in our consciousness. If problems seem to come from every direction, no matter how small each dilemma, pay attention! Spirit is saying it is time for creative thinking. Dr. Raymond Charles Barker taught that the solution to any difficulty is as near as your next thought, since all ideas of Infinite Mind are just waiting to be claimed.

> *There is a Power in me, acting through me, and acting for me which causes me to accomplish what I want.*
>
> —Dr. Raymond Charles Barker
> The Science of Successful Living

If life seems as static as a tape playing the same tune over and over and over, you are ripe for unhappiness. Lazy thinking and a lack of creativity are very destructive, not just to ourselves, but to everyone in our environment. Sometimes we are under the delusion that our husband, wife, children, or the neighbors are the problem. Our world today is so full of opportunities for learning and growing, giving and loving, we have no reason to be unhappy or bored. Being excited about life is a spiritual necessity, but sometimes it requires that we consciously decide to make it happen.

In metaphysics we know that through the use of affirmative prayer we can demonstrate greater success and happiness by shifting our limited beliefs and thus have a changed experience. Operation of the Law is easily misunderstood. We are not successful very long if we push through any problem with sheer willpower. Working for success and prosperity by mentally controlling conditions can be dangerous. If we comply with the way the Universe operates, we shall bring greater possibilities and happier conditions into our experience. It does not mean that we get exactly what we want. Holmes is very clear about this, "We not only believe, but we know that it is entirely possible, through mental treatment—through right thought and belief—to greatly influence our environment, its reaction to us, the situations we meet and the conditions we contact." So specifically how do we use this knowledge? We begin with the decision to be happy and then use the process of disciplined inquiry to explore our consciousness and find areas for positive change. The process involved in disciplined inquiry frees our mind and we uncover opportunities to reach new heights in all areas of life.

To review the basic fundamentals operating in the Universe, in metaphysics we've learned that the Spirit of God is a Divine Creative Presence composed of love, and Law operates as a mechanical and impersonal force that can do anything for us that we totally embody and believe. This occurs through what we call the Law of Attraction—we attract that which is like our belief. We unconsciously pour our beliefs into mind, like a jello mold, and as the jello solidifies, we experience form, the replica of our thoughts. Beliefs we hold in mind create the mold for the action of Law to pour in, filling it to the level of our belief.

> *Don't fall into the "miracle trap," for by doing so you will tend to give up control of your life.*
>
> —Eric Butterworth
> The Universe is Calling

The Law has no limit, but our understanding of It appears to be limited. Therefore, if we want the life we desire, we must become more like that. It means we learn to stop our mind from dwelling on thoughts of not enough, too poor, too short, too tall, too…anything. Cut off thoughts focusing on the negative and replace them with positive thoughts, so our life will represent more of what we want. I once suggested to a fellow looking for his right-and-perfect mate that he carry a folded up piece of paper in his pocket for one day, and every time he had a negative thought or said something negative, just casually get out the paper and put a dot on it. A couple of weeks later I asked how the experiment went, and he said by noon there were so many dots on the paper he threw it away, but the point was made. Awareness, recognizing our negative patterns, is a major step and can be very humbling.

Isn't it a fascinating predicament that what we want will show up when we transform ourselves into the thing itself! So, if we want a friend, be a friend. If we want more love, give more love. Although there is only One Law, the way it applies to different areas of our life can be more easily understood when we use other titles for it. For instance, in describing how we attract things and people to us is more easily understood when we call it the Law of Attraction. When we become the attributes of the thing we want, the Law of Attraction brings it into our life. Can we consciously make this work in an even greater way? Yes, it's really not complex, but it can be challenging and requires that we honestly inventory our beliefs. For example, single adults often focus a lot of energy on finding their right and perfect mate, many times hoping that person will compensate for their lack of something. The goal of finding a mate can become such an obsession that it can reach a point where every time they meet someone, mind says, "Is this it?" Often lists are made detailing the exact specifications of a perfect mate, but too often the lists contain descriptions of form, such as height, weight, hair color, hobby, etc. Then the ideal looking person shows up, usually with negative personality traits. The most effective list contains personal attributes, such as loving, honest, joyful, supportive, playful, sincere, etc. Yet the truth is, until the list-maker expresses more of the attributes on the list, the ideal mate can be an illusive dream. Relationships show up that may not match the list, but are a mirror of where the list-maker is in their understanding of life.

> *If one desires a particular experience, one should seek the causes that would give rise to it, and if one does not desire a particular experience, like pain or suffering, then one should ensure that the causes and conditions which would give rise to it no longer arise.*
>
> —The Dalai Lama
> Healing Anger

Comparing the attributes of whatever we want, whether it is a car, home, or job, with an honest appraisal of how well we embody these attributes, clearly defines the areas we should consider in our personal growth program. The attribute of a car may be freedom; a home may be security; a job may be prosperity. If these attributes are really important—are they important enough to embody ourselves?

Since Law is creative and impersonal and responds to us perfectly every time, we cannot demonstrate anything that is love if our thoughts are based on its opposite, fear. How can we demonstrate freedom if our thoughts are based on bondage? Another way of looking at this is through the Law of Mental Equivalents. We experience the equivalent of our (mental) beliefs. As it says in the Bible, "Whatsoever a man soweth, that shall he also reap." This is another indicator that when we do anything negative, physically or in mind, it comes back to us because it is the Law. And yet it can take years or even decades to reach a clear enough understanding of this principle before we choose to shift away from negativity in our thoughts, words, or deeds. This does not mean we should bury negative thoughts, but instead, open up to a different way of thinking through contemplation and meditation and use affirmative prayer to shift that understanding. Jesus understood this power. He had a great sense of Oneness and alignment with the Divine Presence and understood the Universal Law of Mind. He gave thanks and commanded the Law to work, and it did. Holmes explains, "Practice is a definite statement in mind, a positive affirmation. It is an active, conscious, aggressive mental movement and in such degree as it embodies an idea—and there is no longer anything in our minds which denies the idea—it will take form, because it now becomes a part of the law and order of the Universe in which we live." Our problems are primarily mental and the answers are found in Spiritual Realization.

One area where the Law of Mental Equivalents can be seen is health. All things respond to mind, including our health. Our body is an effect, not a cause. Through affirmative prayer health problems can be corrected, but there are many people who cannot be helped or healed through mental means because they will not take the responsibility of making their own decision for health. Maintaining health, just like any other aspect of our life, takes determination. Decide if you want to continue creating the results of negative beliefs, and if not, let them go. If we do not give our attention to negative thoughts and pray that our life is positive and life affirming, the old beliefs will leave and take along with them the resultant negative experiences. This doesn't mean we never have another negative thought, but when it shows up, we notice and immediately stop it, ideally in mid-sentence.

Either you act with authority upon your world, or your world will give you an average existence.

—Dr. Raymond Charles Barker
The Science of Successful Living

Since we have been given the freedom to choose, we can go either in the direction of an upward expanding spiral of expression, the essence of God, or against it. Holmes explains that the criteria for deciding what is right or wrong is not found in someone else's opinion, but in asking a basic question: "Does the thing I wish to do express more life, more happiness, more peace to myself, and at the same time harm no one?" If the answer is yes, then it is the right thing to do. Any time we do something that holds us back or is at the expense of someone else, it is the wrong use of the Law and we will pay the consequences. We pay the price in both mental and spiritual coin. We always reap what we sow.

We begin disciplining the mind by being consciously aware of negative thoughts. The most effective way to do this is in meditation. As we still the mind, thoughts come barging in, which is the perfect time to recognize patterns of thinking. Just pay attention and let the thought pass on by without judgment. It is never too late to begin mental discipline. We cannot demonstrate freedom if our focus is on limitation. The rewards are great and the good news is that we have been given an unlimited capacity for improving our lives by this method. This does not mean we deny thoughts and feelings. It is by looking, seeing, and noticing our thoughts that we recognize there is something greater and kinder we can do for ourselves. As Raymond Charles Barker wrote, "It is time to cease being content with the average, and with deliberate intent choose creative ideas and hold them close to you until they are subconsciously established and the law of mind brings them into fruition." Deliberately choose to replace negative thoughts with positive ones. As we discipline our conscious mind, the Cause of our experience, we will have a disciplined experience. Trust this…it is the nature of Law to work; it is not up to us to make it work. Have the confidence of spiritual teachers throughout the ages who knew that our success and happiness is dependent on our present attitude.

> *Meditation stills the wandering mind and establishes us forever in a state of peace that remains stable no matter what happens around us.*
>
> —Swami Muktananda
> Where Are You Going?

In the rules of the game of life, to be more, see more, experience more success and happiness, we have to look inside, be honest and take action. In metaphysics it is often said, "Treat and move your feet." Do an affirmative prayer (spiritually treat the mind) and then take action. The following points are powerful action steps to put Law in motion. They can be used together or individually. Our co-creative nature and the Universe will support you—-it's the Law. Let's begin: 1) Decide to be happy. Know you have the right to be happy and Spirit, God, the Universe supports you. 2) Stop telling anyone, including yourself, that you are not happy. This only reinforces the pattern. 3) See the good in life. Even the smallest positive act of children, co-workers, spouses or friends should be praised. Loving words allow you, as well as others, to see the beautiful part of you. 4) Catch any negative mind chatter and stop it mid-stream, replacing it with positive verbal statements. Verbal expressions carry more forceful energy. 5) Do something new or different. Get out of any rut and expand your horizons, whether in creative endeavors, new friends, new food, or new books. Enlarge your life. By taking action in any of these areas, expands your circle of experience. Each time we expand our circle, our life experience expands and things that may have seemed challenging in the past are now not so difficult. We start each day in a new place where we are greater than the day before.

It has been trendy these past twenty years or so to be blatantly honest and let out our feelings, not repressing thoughts about what we feel. But throughout history sages have taught the power of quieting the mind, disciplining the mind, strengthening the mind, and therefore freeing the self. The more we reinforce negative thoughts by acting them out, the more challenging it is to find inner peace. Desires and emotions come in an endless stream and by using spiritual techniques we can sort them out.

One of the things Ernest Holmes made clear is that we are not here for the purpose of making an impression upon our environment, but instead, we are hear to express ourselves in and through our environment. At first this may seem to be in conflict with the tradition of establishing goals and dreams, but what he is saying is that it is not necessary when we die that our obituary makes the headlines or is even two sentences long in the newspaper. He says, "All that means anything is that while we live, WE LIVE, and wherever we go from here we keep on living." Think about this…and a burden is removed. Holmes says, "We don't have to move the world—it is going to move anyway." The Universe, Spirit, God, supports us, because in doing so It expresses even more fully. This is why you are the Precious One in whom God is well pleased. Express yourself today in joy, love, happiness, and success. This is your purpose. Begin today.

> *The mind is the source of both bondage and liberation, the source of both sorrow and joy, our worst enemy as well as our greatest friend. That is why, if there is anything worth knowing in this world, it is the mind.*
>
> —Swami Muktananda
> Where Are You Going?

DIALOGUE

I think I have found my perfect relationship. We love being together, having fun together. The only problem is that I really resist telling this person about my past. I am a different person now, I think, and I want them to see me in this way. What should I do?

It is so interesting when we think we have met the person of our dreams, but we hesitate to be totally honest and open with them. There is tremendous power and grace flowing through our life when we maintain integrity in everything we do. Integrity is the foundation of our life. If we build a house, a job, a relationship on anything less than total integrity, we are constructing life on a foundation of sand. Begin now to be honest with this person. If they can honor your past and love you in the present, you have found a wonderful relationship. If they cannot, they will leave. When you are the real you in relationship and they are their real self, you will both find tremendous joy and happiness.

There are so many things in my past that have jaded me from believing that I really can do something worthwhile. I would love to be a writer, but when I try to concentrate, I am haunted by parents who admonished everything I did. It seems I am more and more creative in avoiding what I really desire...to write and share who I am. Any suggestions?

Begin life in this moment! This very moment is real and alive. Everything in the past is just that, the past. Until this moment we have been affected by what people said or did to us in the years gone by, but now is all we have. Right now say to the Universe: I am a successful writer. I give of myself and all I know to the Universe. Recognizing that I am supported in all I do, the Universe supports me in this endeavor. The past is not a precedent for the future. I begin right where I am in an awareness of newness, freshness, and love. I am free to be the real me, right here and right now. Nothing will stop me. And so it is.

AFFIRMATIVE PRAYER

I ACCEPT MY GOOD

God is the only Power behind all creation. This is the source of my Power and it creates everything in my life through the power of my mind. Because I accept that all things come from the One Source, I realize that Divine Joy is my true nature and expression.

Today I accept and believe for myself that I am empowered and totally capable of recognizing all of the good available to me. What I desire is clearly viewed in mind. I am free of doubt, fear or anger, and my focus is on what I truly desire. As I clear away any uncertainty or confusion, I see my life as Divinely Inspired. God has intended that I have everything that I need to create and experience a life of peace, plenty and joy.

To live in joy is my divine inheritance. I release any false restrictions on my life because I am free to be me. I do not have to manipulate, control or struggle. I just let go and allow the solution to appear. What may have seemed mundane in my life now takes on the grandeur of the Presence of God. I do not effort; life is the essence of God. I am awake, alive, aware, and I fully recognize the grace of God in my life.

I am blessed knowing that I have been made in the image and likeness of God, and my actions speak louder than words. My faith in the unseen good sets the Law of Mind into constructive action, and my prayers are answered. I accept God as the Divine Motivator in my life and it demonstrates for me as a profitable life, well-lived and well-loved. I accept this as the Truth for myself and everyone in my environment. I rejoice at the abundant blessings in my life. And so it is. Amen.

Lesson Nine: Our Relationship With The Universe

The topic for this chapter brings to mind that feeling of awe and wonder that comes from laying in the grass under a clear night sky observing the dazzling brilliance of millions and millions of twinkling stars. It is a feeling of awe, reverence and peace, as the mind goes blank, not clinging to any specific thoughts. Something feels right with the world.

It is those moments we want to recapture time and again. In metaphysics we learn that we have the ability to achieve those moments not by pulling back from life, but by allowing our true spiritual nature to surface from deep inside. Daily spiritual practices help us recognize the presence of God in every moment. The more frequently we give ourselves the gift of being in the present moment, we give ourselves a greater opportunity to again feel awe, reverence and peace.

In creating the Universe, God created us through the mechanism of evolution to be spontaneous individuals and then left us alone to awaken ourselves. At a spiritual level we are all one, yet life looks so different to us on the outside. As an example, think of a colorful balloon bouquet. The air in each balloon is the same, yet on the outside each one is different in color, shape and size. If we break a balloon, all of the air merges with "the air," the Oneness, yet for awhile each one appeared different to us. Looking at this spiritually, if we were a balloon we might judge other balloons by their color or stature, yet we would have the ability to find out that on the inside, we were alike. We would not have to wait until our outer shell burst and we again became one with the air to discover our unity, but it would be our choice. Like a balloon, when our outer shell bursts, we die and again become one with the Universe. If we learn and understand our true nature while we are still here, life can be a blissful experience. As we grow in our understanding, we take the new knowledge with us as we make our transition—our outer shell bursts and we move on.

> *We are bound by nothing except belief. Everything we experience, touch, taste, handle and smell—environment, bodies, conditions, money, happiness, friends—are all effects.*
>
> —Ernest Holmes
> The Science of Mind

Another way of looking at this is to see big balloons and little balloons as the trials and tribulations in life. A few balloons must burst before we understand that it is our negative beliefs and experiences that are holding us back from knowing the truth and enjoying life at a higher level. Every time we break a balloon and find only Oneness, we get stronger. "Behold I stand at the door and knock..." Contact with Spirit, God, Universal Oneness is there awaiting our recognition, but it means a few balloons must pop along the way.

Life is in harmony with all creation and as such, is continually evolving, just like the continuing evolution and expansion of the Universe. We evolve in our understanding that harmony, love and peace bring more positive experiences in our life, and as we embody or reject those traits it impacts others. In this way we make a positive or negative impact on the Universe as a whole. On the path of discovery, our spiritual muscles get strengthened, one way or another. We suffer to the degree that we are not aligned with the Law, which simply says, what we give we receive—what we sow we reap. We create our own experience, which can be heavenly or just plain hell. How often do you have a day like that? When we use the Law negatively, we suffer accordingly. Suffering is not pre-ordained; the intensity of our belief is key to our degree of suffering. We have been blessed with the freedom to make choices, and God has given us the power to back it up. "Fear not, little flock, it is your Father's good pleasure to give you the Kingdom." It is up to us as individual beings to learn how to activate the Kingdom.

> *Each is drawing from Life what he thinks into it. To learn how to think is to learn how to live. Man, by thinking, can bring into his experience whatever he desires if he thinks correctly. This is not done by holding thoughts, but by knowing the Truth.*
>
> —Ernest Holmes
> The Science of Mind

Can you recognize even one thing that happened to you this week that is the result of seeds sown earlier, last week or a year ago? Would you say you were less aware of your use of the Law at that time? If so, what a beautiful expression of evolution for you! We learn by trial and error or more gracefully by the assistance of spiritual teachers, like Ernest Holmes, who wrote "we are not punished for our sins but by them." This may be good news or bad news, but it is true. As individuals it is up to us to mentally lift ourselves above the Law of Averages and reach a higher understanding of Spirit and Law. In the Law of Averages, if we choose not to work for a greater understanding and a more positive life experience, we get "potluck" and the result is an average existence. By studying spiritual laws and using this knowledge, we will not have a "potluck" life.

If all it takes is a little effort, why wouldn't everyone live a heavenly life? We let ego and willpower tip the scales so that we think brightly colored balloons are goals in and of themselves. In life experiences there are three actors: the changeless Self, which doesn't shine as brightly as it could due to negative aspects of our personality; the individual ego and how we identify ourselves; and this sense of separateness, the illusion that adds confusion and holds us back from self-realization. Part of the power of self-will comes from our five senses. Outer experiences have a great hold on our quest for knowledge and beliefs.

To make sense out of this, it helps to begin by developing a greater understanding of why we are here. In the sacred text, the *Upanishad*, it says that as a spider weaves a web out of itself, God weaves the web of the Universe from Itself. When Holmes wrote, "the nature of God is reenacted through us," he meant we are part of this web of life, that our nature is identical with God's nature, because we are God's divine creation. The Universe is nothing but the play of God's energy. God as the Universe in full expression is vividly described by astronaut Edgar Mitchell in his book, *The Way of the Explorer*. He writes, "We've discovered that matter is interconnected and 'resonates' in some mysterious manner throughout the entire universe, and patterns repeat themselves as though a template were being used over and over again on different scale sizes." Through the "butterfly effect" he describes the impact our individual decisions have on everything, large or small, just as minute changes in the atmosphere can dramatically change a weather pattern. Patterns in our life repeat themselves, but it is our personal choice and belief that influences their direction. Like Holmes and Troward, Mitchell writes that life itself is the only vehicle for learning. He believes this is true not only for us, but for the Universe as a whole. He believes each life expresses one of nature's emergent potentials that may prove significant for the whole of creation.

> *The difference between existence and knowing must be carefully observed when considering the larger viewpoint.*
>
> —Dr. Edgar Mitchell
> The Way of the Explorer

Do you ever wonder what the world will look like in one hundred years? If we understand the evolutionary concept, we can see that as a civilization we ultimately become the essence of our deepest intent. By using our individual intent we help direct this evolving pattern. Each one of us has the power to make a difference in this lifetime. It does not take tremendous effort or energy. We can conserve our energy immensely through the simple process of turning our attention from ourselves and directing it to the needs of others, for when we are poor on the outside, we are also poor in thoughts and beliefs.

Will science ever discover an accurate model of the workings of the Universe? Mitchell thinks not, because the mind, our mind, is a continually evolving product of nature that will never totally understand how and why God expresses. We do know that with effective prayer, affirmative prayer, physical changes do occur because in this fluid environment, the Oneness, our mind can change the effects, the results. If our individual mind can do that, what power we have! Remember the Berlin Wall? When the consciousness of freedom in that population became so strong, the walls of imprisonment literally came down. The evil attitude of the East German government was not an evil thing in itself, but a simple a misuse of the Law of Freedom. Like any destructive experience, evil disappears when we no longer indulge in it.

All planets, stars, space…everything at some level is expanding and creating, which requires a level of intention behind it. It is awe inspiring to think of the Universe as perfection evolving, yet it can be difficult to see perfection in daily life as we experience loss, perceive lack, and observe violence in our communities and around the world. Thomas Troward described the Universe as an upward spiral into infinity. We can actually observe this spiral, this shift from lower to higher levels of consciousness in society as a whole. We witness the potential possibility of what we call the highest and the lowest in everything, even though it is all the same thing functioning at various levels.

Thought becomes subjectified in Mind like a seed planted in the soil, and unless neutralized, it stays there and determines the attraction and repulsion in the experience of the one thinking. We, and we alone, control our destiny.

—Ernest Holmes
The Science of Mind

In *The Science of Mind*, Holmes says, "Nothing could give form to a formless stuff, which has no mind of its own, but some Intelligence operating through it." The lowest level is atomic intelligence, physical things such as rocks, trees, dirt. Next is the simple consciousness we find in the animal kingdom, followed by personal consciousness, which we also experience in degrees, and eventually Cosmic consciousness. From one end to the other, all is perfect—all will eventually move up the scale no matter how erratic or slowly each one progresses. It has been said that a cloud cannot obscure the sun forever. We cannot obscure our true nature forever. Eventually all forms of life will see the sun and reach Cosmic consciousness, and the degree to which we develop our personal consciousness in this lifetime is how we influence this process.

The conclusion of experiments studied by Mitchell, suggests that all of nature is in a sense wavelike, field-like and mind-like and that nature's energy moves forward through irreversible processes on a macro level. At this level the processes of decay and creation operate continually, moving forward (i.e. Troward's upward spiral), all without a loss of energy on the microscale. We know that in every moment we are either the creators or destroyers of our heavenly experience, which is why I find Mitchell's theory, which he terms the Dyadic Model, helpful. It is a more technical understanding, which gives greater definition to metaphysics and co-creation, yet no model is big enough to include the Truth. We know by experience that as we correct errors and shift to a more positive way of creating joy in each moment, our life experience improves. In this model the Universe does the same thing at a fundamental level; the Universe learns through a feedback loop process. If the earth is eventually blown apart by nuclear weapons, the Universe learns and shifts, and will continue evolving on a new and more successful path.

Nature stores information about the success of any plant, animal, etc., in a variety of ways, such as in DNA. Through this information storage process, the Universe receives information on the success and failure of cells or species. Adaptation occurs and onward and upward it goes. But how does the Universe learn? Mitchell proposes that learning requires both a level of awareness and intention. He says that awareness without intention is immobile—nothing happens. Intention without awareness is blind, and on top of that, without memory, it would be pure chaos. So if awareness, intention and memory are needed in order to have progress, what we have is not just volitional humans, but at a cellular level we have a volitional Universe. Just as we learn and improve through success and failure, so do all processes in the Universe, which for us means over time the human race does improve its social well-being.

Plotinus tells us that there are three ways by which we gather knowledge: through science, opinion, and intuition or illumination. Each is an avenue leading to self-knowingness and self-knowingness is the very nature and essence of Spirit. The whole nature of God as we understand it, is reenacted through us. In our small world we have volition, the choice of individual expression, yet our basic nature comes from God. This is what Jesus meant when he said, "As the Father hath life within Himself, so hath He given to the Son to have life within himself." A drop of water from a faucet is not the whole ocean, but does have within it the same attributes and qualities of the water in the ocean. All experiences in our life contain the same attributes and qualities of our source, our Divine Source. Whether we choose paths of destruction or creation, the essence of our being remains the same. We are individuals who choose consciously, with complete freedom, how life will be and we have the power of the Universe to back it up. Nothing is going to happen to us that does not happen through us. As we embody the principles of metaphysics and perfect our use of affirmative prayer, we can change the expected result of our causation.

> *The encouraging message is by consciously knowing that there is no inherited tendency toward limitation, no race suggestion operating through subjectivity, nothing in, around or through us that believes in or accepts limitation in any way, shape, manner or form.*
>
> —Ernest Holmes
> The Science of Mind

If we were only given the opportunity to dream about freedom, we would forever be in bondage. But we have freedom—freedom to suffer or to not suffer. Freedom implies there is the possibility of suffering, because we are free to choose more than one course of action at any time. Holmes says we will cease to suffer as we find ways to more completely embody and comply with the Laws of the Universe. We will arrive at this consciousness to the degree we recognize that "what we are looking for, we are looking with." Both heaven and hell are states of consciousness. Jesus said, "As thou hast believed, so be it done unto thee." All suffering is the result of some violation of the Law and these limitations are unnecessary.

At the same time we must know definitely and consistently the Universe is for us and not against us. We know this because we understand we have the freedom to do, say, and think as we wish and to express life as we desire. To just think about being free would not be freedom. On the soul side of life, we are subconscious, not unconscious. Our subconscious is compelled to create what we put into it. Soul not only receives the seeds of our thought, it contains our inherited tendencies—race consciousness. Holmes explains, "The soul is the creative power within us, creating from the patterns given it, and from the memories it contains." He goes on, "The soul, being the seat of memory, already contains a record of everything that has ever happened to us. These memories as a whole constitute the subjective tendency of the individual life, which can be changed through constant effort and a determined persistency of purpose. The soul life of all people is the collective unconscious and is a powerful race suggestion."

With the increasing acceptance of metaphysics in the world, more people are realizing we have learned all we need to through suffering and pain. God could not wish us to suffer, but at this level of awareness, gives us the ability to create our individual life experiences. We move forward at our level of understanding, learning from our mistakes as we make the great discovery of our true perfection for ourselves. Jesus said, "Fear not, little flock, it is your Father's good pleasure to give you the Kingdom." A very powerful way to connect with this kingdom is through spiritual practices. Mitchell writes, "Whenever successful meditative disciplines are employed in the pursuit of insight, they result in reduced stress, an elevated sense of calm, buoyed spirits, a greater awareness of synchronous events, and a heightened receptivity to nonlocal information."

> *If you want to know God, theories and speculations are of no use. He is perfectly manifest, but in a subtle form. He is the Unmoving foundation of all our actions, inward and outward.*
>
> —Swami Muktananda
> Play of Consciousness

An example of spiritual realization is found in the book, *To Love Is to Know Me*, by Eknath Eswarren. He shares his personal cosmic experience, "Light pervaded everywhere in the form of the Universe. I saw the earth being born and expanding from the Light of Consciousness." In this moment he realized there are no specific goals and no limitation in life. Maybe this is what John meant when he wrote, "You will know the truth and the truth will make you free." John 8:32. We are free to just be. This is why Holmes taught it is not necessary when we die that anyone ever knew we lived…but while we live, we live!

Since the essence of God is love, we have a natural tendency to do good, yet we are not bound by a rigid mold that limits our capacity to grow. We can change ourselves completely if we really want to. Often what really limits us is a lack of willpower to see a bigger picture, to see the forest for the trees. If we cannot seem to overcome a craving, we give into an indulgence that leaves us vulnerable to "every wind that blows." In understanding the Law, the way the Universe operates, we are reminded again that we are bound by our beliefs. Heaven and hell are the experiences we have, based on our states of consciousness. Know that the human race believes more in good than in evil, otherwise it would not continue to exist.

The next time you lay in the grass looking up at the stars, know all is right with the world. When we fully express the love in our hearts and the talents we have, the spiral of evolution is lifted for all of humanity. Begin today.

DIALOGUE

In my stressful workday, worrying about bills, my wife and my children, I often wonder why I can't seem to feel happy with life. I use to be happy all the time, but lately I feel like I'm just plodding along and one of these days I'll die wondering if it was all worth it. Any suggestions?

One of the most honorable paths in life is that of the householder, the husband/wife and children. The complexities of the relationships in a family add to the personal and spiritual growth of each individual in unique ways. If we ever wanted to know how we are doing, we look at our spouse and children to find our next area of attention, to continue the expansion of our soul. Is it worth it? Oh, yes, and more, but it takes being awake to the newness of these relationships each day. When we feel like life is getting boring, we may be pulling ourselves back from complete immersion in relationships; we may not be giving enough of ourselves to others in order to receive the love and feedback so important in relationships. Take a few minutes to think about this and then how you can express joy and love in a new way today. It won't take long to experience the rewards.

AFFIRMATIVE PRAYER

LOVE IS THE ONLY POWER

There is a Perfect Intelligence that operates in the Universe. It is the One Source that is eternally manifesting an abundance of goodness and love, always giving of Itself to Its creation. Today I celebrate the privilege of being an active co-creator with the One Source. My life is a part of this One Life of God and there is never anyplace where I am not one with It.

In this knowing, I accept for myself a level of peace and calm that allows my mind to be quiet and center itself on love. I am here to give and receive love and recognize that when I live according to the Law of the Universe, as I give, I receive. I have faith in this Power greater than I and know that my life experiences are the result of my use of the Law. It is the Truth and by understanding this truth, I feel free. My life shines brighter and there is joy in my heart.

I celebrate my Divine potential to think, be, and create greater love in this world. There are no limits on love. As I permit a life of love to express through me, I witness its joy and realize its peace. Any sense of lack or limitation, known or unknown, is dissolved through this strong feeling of love as I move forward into a richer experience of life.

I give great thanks for the realization that I am loved. Love flows into my being and my world. I acknowledge and accept it. I live to give and receive it. Each day is a new adventure in discovering my divine heritage. I move with confidence, knowing that God and all of God's creation is love. I treasure this reality and let this peace fill my soul. I simply let it be, and so it is. Amen.

Lesson Ten: The Atmosphere Of Our Thought

In this chapter we journey into the power of our thought. It is sometimes difficult to imagine thoughts connecting with Universal Mind, creating and bringing things, experiences and people into our lives.

If you strolled through a county fair, walked up to a stranger and told them it was the power of thought that brought you together today, what would they say? Wouldn't it be great if they turned with a smile and said, "Namaste to you, too!" But for most people, thought, whether its power is grasped at all, is focused on getting the best parking space, being first in line, getting the right seat, finding the nicest restaurant, and so on. It is not surprising that one reason people are attracted to metaphysics is to learn how to use the power of their thought to get something. It is a power; yes, it can be directed; yes, it can change our lives for the better. This understanding is a great beginning, but thank goodness it is not the end. There is so much more.

> *We believe what we experience, but we often forget that we experience what we believe.*
>
> —Dr. Stuart Grayson
> Spiritual Healing

For decades we have heard the phrase, "As a man thinkest in his heart, so is he." This is in the Bible, but it also comes to us from great thinkers throughout history, such as Shakespeare, Aristotle, and Greek philosophers. Modern teachers say, "What you believe, you can achieve." This may sound quaint, but Ernest Holmes was very clear, "The united intelligence of the human race could not make a single rosebud; but our thought, centered in Mind, is using the Creative Power of the Universe." It is a spiritual truth, yet throughout history few have used this information for the greater good.

Popular teachers such as Larry Dossey, Deepak Chopra, Thomas Moore, Ken Wilbur, Ram Dass and others, have shown that physical change by spiritual means is a fact. Fungus will grow faster with prayer. Research shows there is an unexplained Infinite Intelligence operating here. And metaphysics teaches that we experience the world of effects because the power of our thought acts in accordance with Law. The Universe responds to us according to Law by corresponding on the outer to what we believe on the inner. This is why when you seek the assistance of a practitioner of metaphysics, one of their first inquiries is to describe what you are currently experiencing in life, because life is corresponding to your beliefs.

Exactly how spiritual healing works we cannot fully understand, but we can deduct why it works. Holmes explains, "The self-knowing of God has the possibility of an eternal expansion. Intelligence responds to intelligence. Infinite Intelligence responds to us by the very necessity of being true to It's own Nature. How does it respond? It can respond ONLY by corresponding. Infinite Intelligence responds by imparting Itself through us." This is why learning the practical application of co-creation in daily life is so powerful. We demonstrate (experience) in our life the correspondence of (that which is like) our thoughts and beliefs. For example, if we fear criticism, we draw people and experiences into our life where there is reason to criticize us. If we fear unstable relationships, experience proves us right. If we fear responsibility, we can find ourselves in situations that demand that we take responsibility combined with negative consequences if we don't.

> *God's work is done, finished and complete, but it is unfolding to our conscious awareness in proportion as we learn the truth and how to bring ourselves into harmony with that truth. The next step is not up to God; it is up to you and to me.*
>
> —Joel Goldsmith
> The Art of Spiritual Healing

Although the scientific study of this process is still young in the history of the world, we can clearly see how humanity has misused thought and spiritual laws to create many sad and ugly conditions in the world. The negative consciousness in every society casts a shadow that is always equal to its height and width. This is why the phrase, "Change your thinking, change your life," is so powerful…because it is that simple. The healer, Jesus, presented this same message when he taught the Law of Life, "It is done unto you as you believe," and not any other way. It takes effort to corral our thoughts without bargaining or trying to coerce the Universe. It requires us to embody the attributes of what we want and then consciously let go and allow the Universal Power of Mind to operate through us. Intent is the key. The challenge is to live each moment being aware of what we are thinking and doing; to check in with ourselves and look at our intent, our motivation, to determine if it is based on fear or love.

The Parable of the Prodigal Son (Luke 15:11–32) reflects the role of intention. The parable begins, "A certain man had two sons." This is a way of describing each one of us. We each have self-choice, the possibility of experiencing good and evil. Another way of looking at this is that we have a natural side and an ideal side. The natural side is like the elder son in the parable, who has an ordinary awareness of life and is satisfied to stay at home and serve his father. The younger son is more idealistic. He is full of desire and great ideas, but lacks what we might call common sense. He is not content to just work the farm with his family, but wants to experience more and…be a little radical.

When we look at this closely, the parable still fits life today. When we find ourselves in a situation that is very uncomfortable, something needs to be done. We are called on to make a change. This is like the young son leaving home with half of his father's money. We have a problem; we look for a solution and there are two options: part of us wants to go with the younger son, and part of us wants to be the older son and maintain the status quo.

The prodigal son goes far away and spends all of his money having a great time. But then a mighty famine strikes and he finds himself hungry and desperate. The inner meaning reflects the typical search we go through to find our way back to God, back to our true nature. We make a lot of false starts, wasting time and energy. Finally we realize that life isn't as pure as we would like it to be and our mind is full of conflict. This is the point when we are the farthest away from a conscious realization of our oneness with God.

> *Spiritual wisdom starts the day that we know from now on every discovery is either a discovery of the self or related to the self in the Cosmic Mind. The self must raise the self by the self.*
>
> —Ernest Holmes
> The Science of Mind

Then in the parable, the younger son "came to himself," which is the moment when he suddenly thinks of home. We reach this turning point when we recognize there is something greater going on. With this strength we have the ability to change, to make things different and take positive steps to take charge of our life once again. Once we make the turn, like the prodigal son, we have a new level of awareness. There is great rejoicing when we discover the truth. Just as the father found great joy in the return of his son, God finds great pleasure when we find our way home.

But in the parable, the elder son is not happy and reminds the father of his own virtues and dedication to stay at home and work. But the negative kind of goodness in the elder brother, is not goodness at all. Failure to do wrong is not necessarily doing right. The elder brother accepted the status quo and never looked beyond what he had at the moment, and thus lived a very stagnant existence.

Thomas Troward explains the elder brother limited himself by believing he had no power to take from his father's estate. He thought he had to wait for permission, not realizing his inherent right, as his father's son, to take whatever he wanted. While one son took up the false idea of independence and separated himself, the other believed he had no independence at all. The whole time he lived among riches and didn't understand how blessed he was. This is a great example of the relationship between Individual Mind and Universal Mind. The elder brother assumed he lived in limitation. We know through studying metaphysics that if our idea is limitation, we find limitation everywhere. Instead, by using the atmosphere of our thought we can recognize our oneness with Spirit, with God. This is when we are welcomed back and we receive the fatted calf, the robe and the sandals.

In more recent times, the first large wave of metaphysical teachers appeared in the late 1800–early 1900s. Their focus was primarily on recognition of our oneness with Spirit, with the intent to shift the atmosphere of mind for the purpose of physical healing; to show positive results by using the power of the mind in accordance with Law to heal physical problems. These philosophical teachings came to be known as "New Thought." Its roots in the U. S. were in the New England ideas of Ralph Waldo Emerson and in England, Judge Thomas Troward. New Thought's major proponents were Ernest Holmes, Phineas Quimby, Ralph Waldo Trine, Horatio Dresser in the United States and Thomas Troward in England. The Western healers and teachers most remembered impacted millions of lives—-healers such as Ernest Holmes (founder of Religious Science), Emma Curtis Hopkins, Mary Baker Eddy (founder of Christian Science), Charles and Myrtle Fillmore (founder of Unity), and Raymond Charles Barker (a Religious Science Minister). Yet today it seems as though western minds find it more difficult to believe in the power of mind for physical healing, and it may seem more palatable or easier to explain if the healers are Eastern, healers such as Sai Baba, Neem Karoli Baba, or Swami Muktananda. Yet right now we there are many powerful western teachers and healers. Metaphysics, as taught on the spiritual level, is a healing teaching and there are hundreds of teachers/healers in metaphysical centers and/or churches, who use affirmative prayer for healing on a regular basis. There are hundreds of practitioners, such as those licensed by organizations like the Association of Unity Churches, Religious Science International, United Church of Religious Science, Affiliated New Thought Network and United Divine Science Churches, who have proven to their respective organizations a minimum of three healings in order to be considered for licensing. These are not miracle workers—-it is normal for the power of mind to heal when used in accordance with Law. It is the way life works as **we** guide the atmosphere of our mind and apply spiritual principles through affirmative prayer for the express purpose of healing.

> *Prayer is always answered, but the answer will depend not on what you are hoping to achieve, but on the laws governing the elements you have put together.*
>
> —Eric Butterworth
> The Universe is Calling

Using the atmosphere of our thought for positive results in any area of life is an active process, not a passive one. We cannot sit idly by and expect change to take place. If all we do is abstain from negative thinking, we are not injecting the power of positive thought into the Universe, which is why wishy-washy affirmative prayer brings wishy-washy results. Holmes said, "The first principle fundamental to the understanding of the operation of thought is that we are surrounded by an Infinite Intelligence. This teaching is based on the principle–we are surrounded by an Infinite Mind which reacts to our thought according to Law." It is not up to us to create; we use the power of the One Mind to become, in essence, a co-creator with God.

To become a powerful co-creator, we begin by embodying an idea, convincing ourselves of its certainty. We build a mental equivalent in our consciousness upon which Universal Law will act. This can be done through meditation or contemplation, seeing the results of our idea so firmly planted in the soil, we actually feel assured of the outcome. It is the nature of God to then produce the results. As reflected in Revelations 21:6, "And He said to me, "It is done! I am the Alpha and the Omega, the Beginning and the End. I will give of the fountain of the water of life freely to him who thirsts." God is all that comes between Cause and Effect, which are not two separate things, but one. We set cause in motion with our thoughts and beliefs and we experience the effect, which is always equal to it's cause. This is why in order to achieve an understanding of prosperity, we must first have the consciousness of prosperity, and the same for health, relationships and creativity.

The extent to which we learn to control our thoughts, we will see it reflected in our environment. This is what is meant by the "practical" application of metaphysics. Holmes explains, "Spirit can do for us only what it can do through us. God is personal to us by virtue of being personified through us." The movement of our thought, our consciousness, sets up a shift, a sort of vibration, on the experiences we have in life equal to the depth we have embodied the thought. It works in perfect balance.

> *Faith is the element which transforms the ordinary vibration of thought, created by the finite mind of man, into the spiritual equivalent.*
>
> —Napoleon Hill
> Think and Grow Rich

With this understanding we can look at governments and societies around the world and see the reflection of each society's beliefs. Even the world is a projection of all minds. If world consciousness is fearful and fragmented, we see it in world events. Everyone has the possibility of choice every minute, and with it the liability of experiencing that choice. If this were not the case, we would not be individualized expressions of God. In every moment we reason, choose and direct our mind. During the day conscious mind makes objective choices, such as what to have for breakfast or what clothes to wear. But at night when we are asleep, conscious mind stops and our subconscious mind is in the forefront. During the day subconscious mind is still active, serving us well by keeping our heart beating, controlling our temperature, and maintaining all of the automatic functions of our body. Life would be very short if every breath had to be a conscious decision. At some point we would get distracted or forget to breathe, and that would be it. Thankfully, subconscious mind is our servant forever. Like the electricity in our home, it is always there for us when we need it, and does not care or worry about when we will turn on the switch.

Imagine if everyone in the world had this understanding, that each one of us is a co-creator with Infinite Intelligence! Now this is a thought worth contemplating. Begin today.

DIALOGUE

I am a small businessman that knows how hard it is to succeed in these competitive times. The fear of failure is always there, lurking behind every financial statement. I know spiritually what I believe will eventually show up in my life, but I think fear of failure is also a great motivator in the business world.

Spiritual principles say that if our business transactions are motivated by fear or anxiety, we are placing mines along our path. Success depends on recognizing what we are thinking when we do our work. The effects in your life (business success or failure) are pure consciousness, always. One area to look at is whether your beliefs about how you run your business are based on this fact. Some business people think that by hurting or cheating others it will benefit them. This is pure delusion and they reap the corresponding reward. This may not show up as a business failure, so to speak, but could unfold as a family problem, relationship problem, or personal problem. All areas of your life will be as successful as you believe you will be, honestly.

I get very frustrated when I am trying to believe that I am free, because I feel so trapped at times with work, home, and bills. Other people must feel the same, especially those who are struggling and just getting by.

The most important recognition you can make today is that no matter what the outer experience, you are a co-creator with God and are free to make any decision you wish. Work, home, bills are just corresponding outer effects of the real beliefs you hold. Think about nature and the freedom each animal has to do what they want. Then imagine a squirrel surviving winter if it hasn't spent time storing food for those long cold days and nights. What is freedom? It is a mind set in tune with the greater truth that we are an infinite expression of God. Does this mean life is easy and there is nothing required of us? NO! Our growth, peace, or fulfillment is dependent on our ability to be responsible for our life and those to whom we have made a commitment, such as spouse and children. Freedom is about making choices, and then being the loving, nurturing person who tends to those commitments with love and compassion. This is true freedom; freedom from stress, pain, and suffering. Make a conscious choice today.

AFFIRMATIVE PRAYER

I AM CLEAR

There is a Perfect Intelligence operating in the Universe. It is the One Source that is eternally manifesting in ever-increasing abundance; an abundance of knowledge, freedom and joy. As I am an infinite expression of this One Source, there is an open line of communication to me through my thinking mind and feeling heart. I listen to It, the Infinite Supply of goodness that is always available to me.

Today I am clear that I am a worthy and perfect expression of God. I am in unity with the One. Limitless possibilities are available to me since it is the nature of God to give to Itself continuously. Knowing this Truth, I consciously choose clarity. I gladly drop all doubts and fears and replace them with a deep faith that grows stronger every minute. With this inherent power of Spirit guiding me, I am clear that as I release any and all negative thinking, I make a clear statement into the realm of limitless possibility: My good is here and my good is now. As my loving and personal guide in my life, Spirit supports my choice. Now as I move forward in this new sense of clarity and love, I draw deeply upon the inner flow of God's peaceful presence, this tranquil Power within me.

In great thanksgiving I celebrate and appreciate my divine potential to be and create anything on which I set my mind. Spirit has shown me there is no limit to what my mind can do; therefore, I believe in myself. I believe in my clarity of mind to speak and experience my word as a total experience of the grace of God in action.

Being one with God, I know that all of my needs and desires are provided for, immediately and completely. There is no need to worry. The power of God is my truth and I accept this and embrace everyone in my world in joy and love. And so it is. Amen.

Lesson Eleven: Revitalizing Faith

What is your perspective on life today? Are you happy, sad, bored, indifferent, peaceful, worried? Our perspective controls how we relate to everyone and everything around us and is the primary difference we observe between individuals. So think again, what is your perspective on life today? How much more positive or negative is it than yesterday?

We can tell something about our perspective by noticing how others react when we give our opinion about a situation or event. Our response depends on our perspective at the moment, which may be limitation, temporarily buying into race conscious beliefs, such as "That's impossible," "This is terrible," "I had nothing to do with it." Or we respond from a level of faith that understands the Law of Cause and Effect, "What did I do to deserve this?" or maybe we are in a clear enough place to respond from the mind of a conscious observer, "This is happening for a reason, so how can I best respond?" This response recognizes all experiences as part of our spiritual evolution, calling for greater faith in Spirit, which reflects our consciousness at every moment.

We may find our perspective bounces back and forth between the opposites of lack/limitation to being a conscious observer as we travel this spiritual journey. To the degree we maintain a level of daily spiritual practices and see the presence of God in all activities, is the degree our perspective and reaction to events comes from a deeper level of faith.

If we are to have an active faith—the faith of God instead of merely a faith in God—our thought must be centered in Universal Mind.

—Ernest Holmes
The Science of Mind

It is not unusual that as we feel the peace and calm that comes from being a conscious observer, it is possible to get caught up in the drama of a situation or become distracted by the simplest thing, and then our faith seems to fade. This is why revitalizing faith is a daily practice. It is not enough to read or think about it occasionally. Faith is an active word that requires daily attention in order to keep it strong, so we can maintain the perspective of a conscious observer when life gets challenging.

Faith is also equated with personal power. The greater level of faith we have in ourselves and in the spiritual nature of the Universe, the more power we have in every aspect of life. When our faith is strong there is not much room for worry or anxiety to penetrate our mind. Ernest Holmes wrote, "What is fear? Nothing more nor less than the negative use of faith…faith misplaced; a belief in two powers instead of One; a belief that there can be a Power—opposed to God—whose influence and ability may bring us evil." Misplaced faith shows up as fear that our prayers will not be answered. A feeling of lack is typically based on fear that we are not supported by the Universe. A fear of death is the feeling that eternal life may not be true. What have you been holding onto that can be traced back to misplaced faith about God, Universal Law or eternal life? These are the areas where revitalizing faith can bring greater strength, peace and happiness.

Is fear something to be rid of at all costs? No, because fear can wake us up to options on the path. In Gavin De Becker's book *The Gift of Fear*, he explains that real fear is an evolutionary signal intended to be very brief; a signal that sounds only in the presence of danger, such as the instant fear that comes if we see a big snake while walking in the woods. When ignored, unanswered fear can be very destructive. Yet by watching the evening news it seems that fear is pervasive in all areas of life. De Becker writes, "As human beings, unwarranted fear has assumed a power over us that it holds over no other creature on earth." This is a real problem, because if we hold onto unwarranted fear, there is no space in mind for fear that is intuitively helpful or when there is a risk that needs our attention. DeBecker offers two simple yet profound rules about fear: 1) The very fact that you fear something is solid evidence that it is not happening, and 2) What you fear is rarely what you think you fear—it is what you link to fear. What great insight! How perfect for reflecting on the true nature of our life, God, Spirit, and the Universe. So much of what we call fear (our prayers will not be answered, for instance) is not real fear, because real fear is an involuntary reaction. Instead, what we typically call fear is our voluntary ability, as human beings with the gift of choice, to indulge in anxiety and worry, which doesn't solve anything and, in fact, distracts us from finding solutions.

> *Your undefined desire remains but a longing hope, changing nothing in your experience.*
>
> —Dr. Craig Carter
> How to Use the Power of Mind

We cannot have faith in what we do not understand in some way. As we develop our understanding of the natural laws of the Universe, how mind and Spirit work as one, how life exemplifies our beliefs, we can see that the highest faith is one based on the knowledge that there is nothing to fear. Do you replay "what if" questions in your mind, such as what if my partner leaves me; what if I lose my job; what if…what if…what if? "Faith is the substance of things hoped for, the evidence of things not seen." Hebrews 11:1 Our faith and thought create the mold for our desires to come into being; faith is the critical component of this process. Maintaining and revitalizing faith should not be looked at as a daunting task, but a thrilling experience! Faith allows us to live fearlessly and recognize we are using our co-creative power with God. Now we see what Jesus meant when he said; "And I say unto you, Ask and it shall be given unto you." Matthew 7:7.

The use of affirmative prayer is a very powerful tool for revitalizing faith. It is the means to an end. Affirmative prayer is a mental approach to seeing the truth around us; it defines our thoughts and ideas, which is why it is so effective. The person who has faith in their own ability always accomplishes more than those who lack confidence. This is why people with great faith also have great personal power. Their level of faith is stronger than the circumstances or conditions around them. Their belief in goodness is greater than what appears to be. Affirmative prayer revitalizes faith because it is based on the knowledge there truly is nothing to fear. Yet whether we hold a strong positive or negative faith, we are demonstrating our co-creative power with God. The degree of faith in our belief is the First Cause of life experiences. It is Law; it is done unto us as we believe.

If affirmative prayer is so powerful, why does it often appear not to work? Affirmative prayer manifests our level of spiritual understanding, so as we review our expectations and how life is working for us right now, we ask…is our belief in goodness greater than any appearance of its opposite? Is there some level of belief in duality lingering in a side pocket of our mind? Has a past experience set a precedent, a limitation in our mind? Is there any place where fear or confusion tenaciously hang on? Holding on to any doubt or belief in limitation is a faith in duality and promotes suffering. Holmes says, "All human misery is a result of ignorance; and nothing but knowledge can free us from this ignorance and its effect." Ignorance is the belief in limitation or anything less than the belief that God is love; God is all there is and we are part of that. Anything less "divides our mental house against itself." Strong faith is built from a foundation of belief, acceptance and trust. It is not necessarily instantly achieved, but grows through knowledge and experience. Our path in life is a road of self-discovery that continues without end. How many of us, when asked if we would like to be 21 years old again, say "yes" as long as we could take our current level of knowledge with us! The beauty of life is that our knowledge continues to grow...forever.

> *Healing has its price, just as seeking to understand the nature of one's consciousness does. What are you willing to give up to meet God?*

We are living in an era where science is now accepting prayer as a healing force. In his book *Healing Words*, Larry Dossey discusses scientific tests on the power of prayer. He describes one form he calls nondirected prayer. This is what we call affirmative prayer, where we have feelings, emotions, and images, but do not focus on specific results or a preferred outcome. Dossey reports, "Based on a large number of tests, when nondirected prayer is answered, the outcome is always in the direction of 'what's best for the organism.'" The experiments led researchers to believe that "An answered nondirected prayer is one in which the organism moves toward those states of form and function that are healthiest for it." And then he clarifies, "What is 'best for the individual' may sometimes involve death, not life." Ann and Barry Ulanov describe in their book on prayer *Primary Speech*, "Prayers are sometimes answered by the experience of more struggle, by being plunged into situations where we must risk more than we ever dared before."

Yes, sometimes illness is the vehicle through which we find a deeper level of faith. How often I have observed people with a serious illness or who have a friend with a serious condition, decide it is time to renew their faith. Illness calls us to redirect our attention from the physical body to our spiritual nature at a time when the mind's focus on the body can be almost overpowering. In her book *Why People Don't Heal And How They Can,* Carolyn Myss describes illness as a spiritual challenge. She feels that focusing on our spirituality during an illness does not reduce our chance of physical healing. It is important to understand that spirituality is first and foremost the path to gain inner strength rather than physical strength. She writes, "Change the emotion, change your energy, changes your biology. If you enter a process of change, you maximize your chances of healing." Without inner strength, gaining physical strength is very difficult. "Healing requires personal honesty, and few things are more intimate." This is why illness is a transforming experience. Illness demands that we pay attention to the mental and physical healing processes. After revitalizing our inner strength, physical healing can certainly follow, but we must remember that whether healing occurs or not can also be part of the process on the spiritual path.

> *Getting to know better the nature of the God who is within reveals your own innate power and allows you to become aware of how you co-create whatever you experience in your life, including your health.*
>
> —Dr. Caroline Myss

During illness, various avenues of medical intervention and changes such as nutrition and lifestyle may all help and should be used. Yet the most effective healing includes relying on spiritual practices to bring the insights we need. Meditation can be a way of enduring the consequences of a disease and healing it by increasing the strength of our faith and trusting the wisdom of our spirit—or it can prepare us for the release of our life, if that is the next step on our path of self-discovery. Ram Dass encourages us to seek enlightenment, a perspective where we don't cling anywhere, not to any person, place or thing. He teaches, "The universe is made up of experiences that are designed to burn out our reactivity, which is our attachment, our clinging, to pain, to pleasure, to fear, to all of it. As long as there are places where we're vulnerable, the universe will find ways to confront us with them. That's the way the dance is designed."

Finding where there is attachment or unwarranted fear and then getting clear about it is the gift a practitioner of metaphysics offers those who request assistance. A practitioner's work is done in their own mind knowing the truth about the person, using affirmative prayer to carve a new road, so to speak, into their consciousness. It is an art, a skill that can be learned and taught. Affirmative prayer is not about change; it is about realization. Holmes taught it as Spiritual Mind Treatment, and explained, "Treatment, in its proper content, is the time, process, and method necessary to the changing and redirecting of our thought, clearing the thinking of negation, doubt, and fear, causing us to perceive the ever-presence of God." There is nothing to be healed, only something to revealed.

Whether our challenge is illness, a relationship, or a job crisis, it is not time to separate ourselves from reality. To continue expanding on the path of self-discovery requires that we face all of our fears…see them, feel them, touch them…knowing the truth: God is all there is. The belief in goodness must be greater than any apparent manifestation of its opposite. Therefore, it is our faith that grows through the knowledge we gain from each experience.

Going beyond illness, another challenge that revitalizes faith is the approach of death. Whether it is our personal death or the death of a friend or relative, it appears so final, its approach stirs the soul of even the hardiest non-believer. We are confronted with the end of ourselves as separate entities. In metaphysics death is a transition, a transformation of one spiritual form to another; the end of one chapter in the soul's experience and the beginning of another, since our present life is the one we came to the last time we died. Our Spirit has been on the path of spiritual evolution for a long, long time, yet it is ego's struggle to hold onto the body and other physical attachments that cause a lot of pain and suffering for the dying person and everyone around them.

You don't see the center of the universe because it's all center.

—C. S. Lewis

The lessons that death brings are very powerful, if it is approached with the knowledge of truth, without fear and confusion. Everything happens for a reason and having faith and trust in that reason makes the impossible quite possible. It is possible to approach death in peace and harmony. Within us is the unborn possibility of limitless experience and we have the privilege of giving birth to it time and time again. The Law of Cause and Effect is not bound by precedent. When we limit our faith to what has already been accomplished, few 'miracles' result. When faith is strong and we recognize our place in Divine Law, there are no limitations, and what appears to be a miraculous result will follow.

A pitfall on the spiritual path is the belief that the correct manifestation of affirmative prayer is a problem always gets better; when we pray powerfully enough, the problem will be solved, the illness will be healed, and many times it is. But the truth is we do not know what the perfect result should be. This is one of the challenges of faith and the power of nondirected prayer. We commune at the level of Universal Mind with Spirit, knowing perfection, wholeness, and completeness, and no suffering is necessary. When my mother was fighting cancer, although I wanted her healed immediately, I recognized her spirit had the power to either let go of past pain and anger and heal, or go on her way, because there was no need to physically suffer. Our family was by her side when the struggle got too much and she left her body quickly. She was my best friend and, by being a conscious observer, I saw her transition as peaceful and beautiful. It was reinforced the next day when I had a vision that was so clear, I could still paint it in detail...she was dancing and laughing with her sister, who had made her transition two years before. Even now, a year later, I periodically start to pick up the phone to call her, and then remember...she is not here, but in the loving arms of God on her next evolutionary journey of the soul.

And so what is your perspective on life now, after reading this chapter? Do you feel a greater sense of the infinite power that resides in you? The depth of our realization that God is all there is strengthens our ability to be a positive, co-creative force in this world; a force not just for change, but realization on a greater level so more people have the faith to tap their true potential in every moment. By revitalizing our faith, we create more beauty, love, and joy for this life and beyond. Rejoice!

DIALOGUE

In a group it always seems that others think I don't know as much as they do, which means I talk less and less, and eventually I become the proverbial wallflower. What can I do to stop this cycle?

Realize other people's opinions of you may reflect your own evaluation of yourself. Healing this incorrect image is the first step in climbing out of the well of self-pity. We can all express a radiance of knowledge, beauty and self-confidence by knowing the truth about ourselves and those around us. Remember the Law of Cause and Effect. When your confidence and faith are strong, it will be reflected back to you through others and those are the friends you will enjoy the most. Use the principles in this lesson to help reactivate or revitalize faith in your self as a worthy, intelligent, loving individual. I know who you really are…a divine expression of the highest and best.

One of my challenges is remembering the truth as I watch the news and major events unfold around the world. It seems that humanity hasn't learned much; we keep repeating aggressive and painful acts and it seems more people feel overwhelmed and care less and less about the outcome. How can I help change these patterns so issues in the world end with a more positive result?

Let's go back to the truth; everyone is sowing and reaping, sowing and reaping. Whether we win the lottery or get mugged, we are reaping the seeds we have sown. Yet we don't need violence or suffering on the spiritual path, so it calls for personal strength and faith to remain sane and know whatever seeds we plant, we will reap. Every time countries go to war, every person involved is there out of their own consciousness. It may be dramatic, sad, and make us frustrated and angry, but there is a purpose and something will be revealed. We have front row seats in the evolution of human consciousness…evolution and growth. It seems like in these past ten years we have come close to being done with war as a society, but it is the whole human race that is trying to grapple with this idea of world peace. By understanding Universal Mind and the power of our thought, we can help end this pattern of violence by looking inside at how much anger, revenge, blame, and war-like consciousness is in each of us. When we can bring peace to ourselves, then we are planting seeds for the rest of the world. We must believe more in the solution than in the problem. Keeping our faith revitalized gives more power to the solution.

AFFIRMATIVE PRAYER

I TRUST MY LIFE

There is only one Mind; this Mind is God; this Mind is my mind now. This is the one and only presence that permeates this Universe. It is the love of God in me, as me, which has created me. I celebrate this truth with positive faith and trust. It conveys a powerful message that although I may not see or understand my destination in life, I clearly know something wonderful is happening right now.

I affirm and accept I am committed to experience consciously the divine presence of God in me, as me. I embrace all opportunities and responsibilities with love. Each person I meet or come in contact with is the recipient of my love, because in great faith Spirit guides me and directs me in perfect right action. Every moment is an opportunity to express the beauty and vitality pulsing within. No former belief can stop the positive movement of creative energy through my consciousness, because I now commit myself to live consistently with the words I speak and the ideas I choose each day. I am lifted to the highest point of perception, where I know how greatly I am loved and how beautifully my life is working. I trust in Universal Goodness.

As I allow this truth to permeate my mind and body, it brings feelings of peace, joy and thanksgiving. I am overflowing with the power of Divine Love moving forward as a force for good in life. My gifts are the gifts of Spirit, to be shared joyously. Gratefully I acknowledge God is all there is and I accept this divine simplicity, releasing concern about all activities in the world. I let God's fullness shine forth in my life and release this word to the Infinite Law of Mind, where it is free to create the results of deep abiding faith and trust. And so it is. Amen.

Lesson Twelve: The Power of Meditation

In pursuing knowledge on the spiritual path, what tools are you using to expand, grow and deepen your understanding? These lessons, along with other readings, attending spiritual centers, church, seminars, lectures and classes are all great spiritual tools. But interestingly enough, we often do not feel closest to Spirit at moments of intense activity, but instead, we find a connection deep inside when we are quiet. Meditation is a powerful tool for expanding the quiet moments when we connect with the sacred, sense deep inner peace, the joy of life without effort, and make space for answers to be revealed.

Meditation, like many other spiritual practices throughout the world, has not been a cornerstone of metaphysics. Yet while the practice of meditation has not been a Western tradition, in most religions or philosophies the power of silence is mentioned. We can feel the strength of Dr. Holmes opinion about meditation as a tool when he wrote, "And so we meditate daily upon the Universe of the All Good, the Infinite Indwelling Spirit, which we call God, the Father, Incarnate in man, trying to sense and to feel this Indwelling Good as the Active Principle of our lives…for there is what we seem to be, and what we really are…and as we daily meditate upon this Indwelling God, we shall acquire a greater mental equivalent." By using both meditation and affirmative prayer, Holmes was confident, "The one who wishes scientifically to work out his problems, must daily take the time to meditate and mentally treat the condition, no matter what the apparent contradictions may be. He is working silently in the Law and the

Law will find an outlet through his faith in It." Silence, meditation and affirmative prayer are a powerful combination.

> *Above all, meditation stills the wandering mind and establishes us forever in a state of peace that remains stable no matter what happens around us. Through meditation we become aware of our fundamental unity with all things.*
>
> —Swami Muktananda
> Where Are You Going

How do we know meditation will be powerful for us? We do not know unless we try it. So how do we begin? Although there is no one right or wrong way to meditate, there are an array of ideas and processes taught around the world that can be used as guidelines. Through the teachings of the illumined the Spiritual Universe reveals Itself and shows to us what we know about God. What we directly experience and what others have experienced, is all we can know about God. Therefore, we learn by studying the teachings of great spiritual leaders throughout history, the mystics, the illumined. Mystics like Jesus, Buddha, and Mother Teresa, were great revealers of the nature of the Universe and our relationship to God. We can learn the basics of meditation by studying their knowledge, their wisdom and methods of connecting with the sacred.

Light comes with an expansion of consciousness. "The light shines in the darkness and the darkness comprehend it not." John 1:5. This pathway of light that is created through the expansion of consciousness, whether it is through affirmative prayer or meditation, is not something we create; it is something that pre-exists and we tap into it. All of the great mystics understood this and the more frequently we tap into it, the greater clarity we will have.

Some of the easier-to-understand teachings about meditation come from eastern mystics. One such mystic, Paramahansa Yogananda, explained meditation is his book, *Journey To Self-Realization*, "Meditation is the concentration upon God. The term is used in a general sense to denote practice of any technique for interiorizing the attention and focusing it on some aspect of God. In the specific sense, meditation refers to the end result of successful practice of such techniques: direct experience of God through intuitive perception. It is the 7th step of the eightfold path of Yoga described by Patanjasli, achieved only after one has attained that fixed concentration within whereby he is completely undisturbed by sensory impressions from the outer world. In deepest meditation one experiences the 8th step of the Yoga path: communion, oneness with God."

> *Superior intelligence was not given to the human being merely to be used to eat breakfast, lunch, and dinner; marry and beget children. It was given that man might understand the meaning of life and find soul freedom.*
>
> —Paramahansa Yogananda
> Journey to Self-Realization

In *The Heart of the Buddha*, Chogyam Trungpa describes meditating as a way to develop mindfulness, which he feels should not be regarded as a minority-group activity or some specialized, eccentric pursuit. "It is a worldwide approach that relates to all experience: it is tuning in to life." This is emphasized in the philosophy of Thich Nhat Hanh, a Vietnamese Zen Master who currently teaches the Four Foundations of Mindfulness at his Plum Village retreat center in France. Here practitioners develop the art of meditating on the mind to be able to see the interdependence of the subject of knowledge and the object of knowledge. He explains that to calm our thoughts we must practice mindfulness of our feelings and perceptions, to know how to observe and recognize the presence of every feeling and thought arising in us. He feels that to receive the full benefits of meditation, we first must build up our power of concentration through the practice of mindfulness in everyday life.

Holmes studied the teachings of Buddha, one of the most well-known teachers of meditation and wrote about him in his book, *The Voice Celestial*:

> Man cannot change the law but he can change
> The sequences. The Noble Eightfold Path
> Will lead to his emancipation, for
> He who fills the stream of consciousness
> With Noble Truths and Love shall cause its depth
> Of waters to run clear: he shall be held
> From pains of guilt, which dying out will set
> Him free to enter in Nirvana.

The Buddha realized the benefit of meditation when he discovered that struggling to find answers did not work. Described by Chogyam Trungpa in, *Cutting Through Spiritual Materialism*, "It was only when there were gaps in his struggle that insights came to him. He began to realize that there was a sane, awake quality within him which manifested itself only in the absence of struggle. So the practice of meditation involves "letting be," trying to go with the pattern, trying to go with the energy and the speed."

In the Siddya Yoga tradition, Swami Muktananda explained that one-pointed concentration is used by everyone at one time or another, such as when we take a test, cook food, or garden. Using this same ability to concentrate and focus on our love for God is meditation, a mind free from thoughts. Another teacher describes it as expanding the space between our thoughts. Through this process we find the place of supreme peace within.

If you meditate on your ideal, you will acquire its nature. If you think of God day and night, you will acquire the nature of God.

—Sri Ramakrishna

The term meditation, as used by Catholic mystics, often refers to a form of prayer where one ponders Christ and, as Carol Lee Finders describes in her book, *Enduring Grace*, "See (the Passion of Christ) as vividly as possible to the mind's eye, moving about from one element to another. The more intensely focused kind of mental activity that constitutes meditation for many of us today is closer to what Catholic mystics would have regarded as mental prayer or interior prayer, which becomes in its most advanced stages, contemplative prayer."

Author's Nick Bakalar & Richard Balkin explain in *The Wisdom of John Paul II,* that although in the Christian tradition there are several definitions of prayer, it is most often described as a talk, a conversation with God. "Conversing with someone, not only do we speak but we also listen. Prayer, therefore, is also listening. It consists of listening to hear the interior voice of grace. Listening to hear the call. And then you ask me how the Pope prays, I answer you: like every Christian—he speaks and he listens. Sometimes, he prays without words, and then he listens all the more. The most important thing is precisely what he 'hears.'"

Although types and styles of meditation vary around the world, any practice of meditation can bring us to that perfect state of awareness over time, where we are just one with everything; we observe without judgment; we sit is smiling repose. Meditation also unleashes in us a tremendous level of peace, love, and compassion. Who wouldn't want more of this in their life! But although meditation seems simple, it can be very challenging at the same time, because we grow as our ability to meditate grows.

When we begin meditating, what tends to come to the forefront of our thoughts is what is described as "the basic neurosis of mind," which is the relationship between ourselves and the world. As we meditate, we begin to understand our thought pattern as well. We see thoughts as just that…thoughts. If we judge our thoughts obsessively, whether condemning or praising, we actually feed and encourage them.

> *Take one slow, deep breath, as slowly and deeply as you can—inhale light, healing, and vitality; exhale and let go—feel a moment of enlightenment.*
>
> —Dan Millman
> Everyday Enlightenment

Chogyam Trungpa describes this process in *The Myth Of Freedom.* "A person always finds when he begins to practice meditation that all sorts of problems are brought out. Any hidden aspects of your personality are brought out into the open, for the simple reason that for the first time you are allowing yourself to see your state of mind as it is. For the first time you are not evaluating your thoughts." Dealing with these thoughts is all part of the process of achieving inner peace.

Ram Dass feels it is important to have some understanding what the game of life is about to want to meditate. This popular American meditation teacher explains the challenge in his book, *Grist For The Mill.* "So we have a little bit of wisdom, and then we try to concentrate. But every time we try to concentrate, all of our other desires, all of our other connections and clingings to the world keep pulling on us all the time. So we have to clean up our game a little bit; that is purification, and then our meditation becomes a little deeper. As our meditation gets deeper we are quieter and we are able to see more of the universe so that wisdom gets deeper and we understand more. The deeper wisdom makes it easier to let go of some of the attachments, which makes it easier to increase right livelihood. All three things keep interweaving with one another; they are a beautiful balancing act." Some people experience the fear of emptiness or nothingness as the mind releases thoughts and there is a moment when we are not relating to someone or something. Although the fear is not real, that sense of floating without a personal identity causes us to hold back. But as the practice continues, we begin to trust the process and ourselves even more.

Many people try meditation to relieve pain, anxiety, tension or sadness. Yet what often comes to mind in the early stages of meditation is the recognition of how protective we are of certain people, places, or things or the particular way we experience life. Every time we recognize another level of attachment in life, we find our growing edge...the next area for more inner work. By continuing to pursue spiritual growth, there will be some point where we suddenly find the hardest work has been left behind. At this point our lessons are easier and our joy more profound.

> *During the experience of pure consciousness the sense of the here-and-now fades away and one experiences a merger with something greater than the individual self...in which the ego and the sense of individual self are transcended.*
>
> —Larry Dossey
> Recovering The Soul

Practicing meditation daily until it becomes a habit is the key. As Yogananda so wisely taught, "Habits of yielding to passions result in suffering. Habits of yielding to the mechanical routine of worldly life beget monotony, indifference, vexation, worry, fear, disgust. Habits of attending church and sacred lectures produce fitful inspiration and momentary desire for God. But habits of devotional meditation and concentration produce realization." This is the gift of making meditation a daily habit.

When we recognize our Spirit is experiencing life through our body for a purpose, we can find out more about our soul's wants, needs and desires through the practice of meditation. Since Spirit is larger than the confines of our body, it is valuable to get more attuned with it, so we can see and understand life from a position greater than what we observe by just being a human being. Our subconscious mind experiences unity with all, contains all knowledge and is the avenue through which we connect with the Divine. We can access this vast library of information and bring it into our conscious mind, and at the same time increase our ability to let intuitive thought surface more easily and clearly to guide us on a daily basis.

Throughout the ages the mystics have taught the value of consciously courting the Divine. Illumination comes as we more frequently realize our Unity with the Whole, and constantly endeavor to let the Truth operate through us. But since we connect with the Whole at the point of our subconscious, it is here alone that we will contact It. Perceiving our Self is somewhat like entering a dark room on a bright and sunny day; it takes awhile for our eyes to adjust. It takes awhile to mentally adjust to meditation so we may experience what lies beyond this physical body and mind.

To assist us in the process, it is helpful to use rituals. Not that a ritual represents any religious belief, but rituals are effective ways to help focus our mind on the inner self. Should you feel any resistance to these suggestions, ignore them, but do not let this stop you from doing basic meditation practices. The most important ritual or step in the process is to find a quiet place to sit where you are not distracted or interrupted. It can be as simple as the corner of a bedroom or study, or in walking meditation using a quiet park, back yard or garden. In sitting meditation, the body position should be comfortable to discourage fidgeting or a desire to sleep. Traditionally this is a cross-legged sitting position with hands in the lap, but you can sit comfortably in a chair or against a wall. The back is held naturally straight without tension, shoulders back. After taking this position several times, the body and mind quickly begin to settle down when you assume "the position," since subconsciously you have accepted this as the beginning of meditation.

There is no greater obstacle to union with God than time.

—Meister Eckhart

Through rituals, the mind soon begins to quiet down as you prepare for meditation. This can enhanced by simply meditating in the same place each day, so as you approach the "place" your mind recognizes it is time to meditate. Having items around that are symbolic of your Oneness also triggers this calming effect. It can be anything that reminds you of your true nature, such as a candle. Perhaps a rock or shell from a special place, or picture of a loved one or spiritual teacher will help the mind to settle down. Creating the atmosphere for meditation can include wearing the same clothing, blanket or shawl for warmth. Each time you put on the clothing, the mind will begin to quiet.

Our goal in preparing for meditation is to create a mind free of all thought, yet fully aware. We let go of memories; we stop creating or solving problems, or dreaming about the future. Our goal is a mind in which we focus on the present, not the past or the future. Meditation is the process of reaching the recognition of the eternal present moment. The good news: it is a process that improves with practice. In the early stages, it is natural to watch the mind become hyperactive at the same time we wish it would calm down. Or the mind finally quiets down and just then a thought comes rushing in, we follow it, and the quietness is gone. Noises or bodily functions can distract us. Many things can take us away from the silence, so it is important to recognize meditation as a process that improves over time.

Various methods can be used to pursue the silence. One of the most traditional is following the breath, focusing on each in-breath and each out-breath. This one-point focus helps us reach that place called the "witness consciousness," where we are just consciously aware of our body functions. This helps us to become the observer so when thoughts arise, we feel no need to cling and can just let them go. Another method to still the mind is repeating one or more words or sounds. In yoga this is called a mantra. Repeating the words "I AM" or a phrase like, "God Is Love," can still the mind and open the heart. Chanting is even a more powerful way to open the heart and tap into oneness. Chanting with a tape in a "call and response" fashion can release tension and build our energy level. There are many chanting and meditation tapes and CD's on the market today. Some are more traditional and create a comfortable sound for those who want to try chanting as a pathway to deep meditation. The chant can be as simple as repetition of the words "Alleluhia," "Kyrie" and "Om Namah Shivaya." Sometimes just listening to the sounds of a Native American pan flute helps me reach that place.

> *We are trying to get peace or happiness from outside, from money or power. But real peace, tranquility, should come from within.*
>
> —The Dalai Lama
> The Wisdom Teachings of the Dalai Lama

The length of meditation depends on the one meditating. Ideally, begin with five minutes and gradually increasing it to 30 minutes a day. If you have the opportunity periodically to meditate more than one hour with a group, it can be a life-changing experience, but for a typical daily practice, 30-minutes is very beneficial.

Signs of progress in meditation include an increasing sense of peacefulness; a conscious inner experience of calmness that expands into bliss; finding answers to questions through the intuitive state; increasing mental and physical efficiency; the desire to hold on to the peace and joy of the meditative state; expanding unconditional love towards our loved ones; actual contact with God, that which is beyond all creation.

Do not to just meditate for meditation's sake, because a passive meditation will never produce an active demonstration, any more than a chef can cook the finest meal by sitting down with his ingredients but never using them. Read, study, think and meditate upon statements which are calming, give us confidence, while erasing all thoughts of fear and tension. The Dalai Lama cautions, "It is easier to meditate than to actually do something for others. But to merely meditate on compassion is to take the passive option. Our meditation should form the basis for action, for seizing the opportunity to do something. The meditator's motivation and sense of universal responsibility should be expressed in deeds."

The result of any spiritual practice is we are called to action. Bless your life and the life of others, your community, and the world by using meditation as a powerful tool for growth and understanding for yourself and others. Begin today.

∞

There is only one Power and one Presence in the Universe. It exists in, as and through everything, so all of creation operates in absolute harmony and balance. Its expressions are limitless and my experience forever reveals this. My true nature expresses Spirit through every aspect of my being, and I move courageously into ever-expanding circles of joy.

Referenced Authors and Publications

Bakalar, Nick and Balken, Richard	The Wisdom of John Paul II
Barker, Dr. Raymond Charles	The Power of Decision
	The Science of Successful Living
	Treat Yourself to Life
Butterworth, Eric	The Universe Is Calling
Carter, Dr. Craig	How to Use the Power of Mind
Cohen, Alan	I Had It All The Time
Dass, Ram	Compassion In Action
	Grist for the Mill
DeBecker, Gavin	The Gift of Fear
Dossey, Larry	Healing Words
Eckhart, Meister	From Whom God Hid Nothing
Einstein, Albert	Ideas and Opinions
Emerson, Ralph W.	Emerson's Essays: Essay on Love and Essay on Self-Reliance
Esswaren, Eknath	To Know Me is to Love Me
Finders, Carol Lee	Enduring Grace
Goldsmith, Joel	The Art of Spiritual Healing
Grayson, Dr. Stewart	Spiritual Healing
Hahn, Thich Nhat	Love in Action

Hill, Napoloen	How to Think and Grow Rich
	Success Through A Positive Mental Attitude
Holmes, Ernest	The Anatomy of Healing Prayer
	Living the Science of Mind
	The Science of Mind
	Observations
	The Voice Celestial
Lama, Dalai	Healing Anger
	The Wisdom Teachings of the Dalai Lama
Lewis, C. S.	
Milliman, Dan	Everyday Enlightenment
Mitchell, Edgar	The Way of the Explorer
Moore, Thomas	Care of the Soul
Muktananda, Swami	Play of Consciousness
	From the Finite to the Infinite
	Where Are You Going?
Myss, Carolyn	Why People Don't Heal and How They Can
Small, Jacquiline	Transformers
Ramakrishna, Sri	
Troward, Dr. Thomas	The Edinburgh & Dore Lectures on Mental Science
	The Law and the Word
	The Creative Process of the Individual
Trungpa, Chogyam	Cutting Through Spiritual Materialism
	The Heart of the Buddha
	The Myth of Freedom

Ulanov, Ann and Barry	Primary Speech
Vahle, Neal	Open At The Top—The Life of Ernest Holmes
Walsch, Neale Donald	Conversations With God, Volumes 1,2,3
Whitman, Walt	
Wilbur, Ken	A Brief History of Everything
	Sex, Ecology and Spirituality
Yogananda, Paramhansa	Journey to Self-Realization
	The Holy Bible, New King James Version

For Metaphysical Classes, Workshops, Seminars

Affiliated New Thought Network 8798 Complex Drive San Diego, CA 92123	www.newthought.org
Association for Global New Thought 1565 Maple Avenue, Suite 205 Evanston, IL 60201	www.agnt.org
Association of Unity Churches 1901 N. W. Blue Parkway Unity Village, MO 64065	www.unity.org
The Emerson Institute P. O. Box 2313 Oakhurst, CA 93644	www.emersoninstitute.edu
Religious Science International P. O. Box 2152 Spokane, WA 99210	www.rsintl.org

United Church of Religious Science www.scienceofmind.com
P. O. Box 75127
Los Angeles, CA 90020

United Divine Science Churches www.uniteddivinescience.org
8419 Callaghan Road
San Antonio, TX 78230

0-595-25415-2